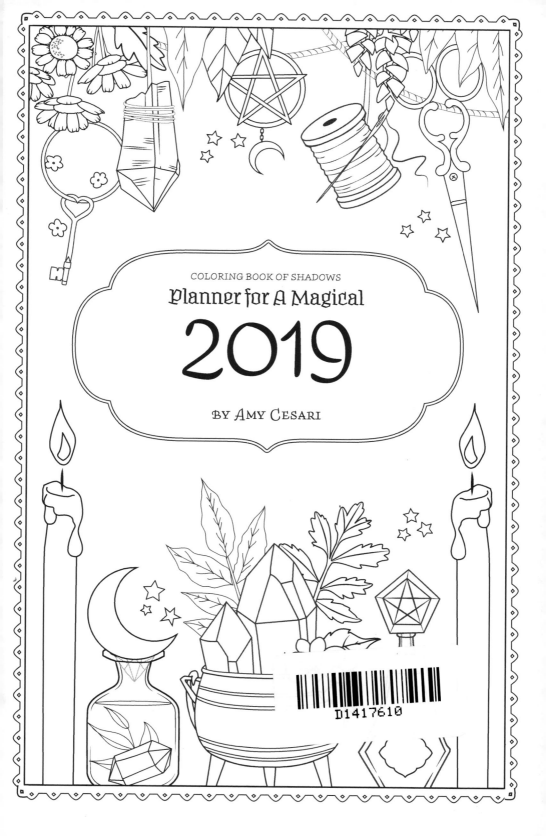

COLORING BOOK OF SHADOWS

Planner for A Magical

2019

BY AMY CESARI

Print and color free pages! Get them at:
COLORINGBOOKOFSHADOWS.COM

Fire Safety Disclaimer:

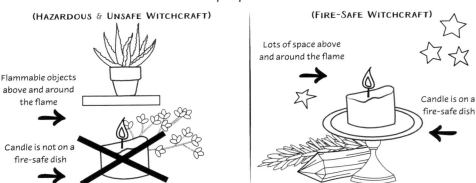

(HAZARDOUS & UNSAFE WITCHCRAFT)

Flammable objects above and around the flame →

Candle is not on a fire-safe dish →

(FIRE-SAFE WITCHCRAFT)

Lots of space above and around the flame →

Candle is on a fire-safe dish ←

The images in this book are for decorative purposes—they are not realistic guides for arranging flame-based altars. Always place a fireproof dish beneath candles & incense. Leave clearance above & around flames. Do not place flammable objects near flames, and never leave flaming things or incense unattended. Users of this book take full responsibility when using fire.

This Magical Year Belongs To:

I Solemnly Swear That I'll Make the Most of this Magical Year

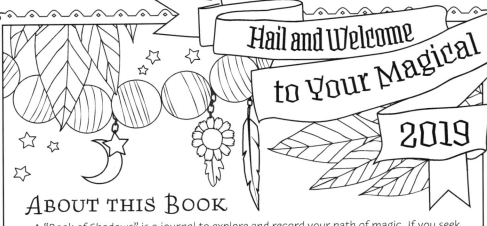

Hail and Welcome to Your Magical 2019

About this Book

A "Book of Shadows" is a journal to explore and record your path of magic. If you seek it, magic will unfold before you in fantastic ways. All you have to do is take the first curious steps and follow where it leads.

As a witch, you can claim control over your own destiny, harnessing intention, will, and natural forces already in play—such as the moon, the sun, and the changing seasons, also known as The Wheel of the Year. These energies can enhance and inspire your spells, and help you make the most of your magic. And so this book is about using the powerful magic found in the seasons, moon, sun, earth, and most important—within your witchy self.

The seasons wield immense power, and you can use this to your advantage with simple shifts in how you plan things in your life. Here's an example. Have New Year's resolutions always felt forced? That's because winter is the lowest point of seasonal and sun energy. Manifesting a significant change is better started in spring when the seasonal energies begin to build momentum for the year. Winter is more optimal for going inward and creating change beneath the surface.

In this book, we'll focus on tapping into the seasonal energy through simple planning and practical witchcraft. You already have what you need to make the most of your magical life. All you have to do is start. And, most of all, have fun!

How to Use This Planner

"An' it harm none, do what ye will!" This is your Magical Planner. There are no rules! It's all up to you. But here are some tips and suggestions:

• The front of this book includes quick reference guides to the Wheel of the Year, Moon Phase, Days of the Week, and other correspondences that you may find useful. It also has tips for using the astrological and moon phase information on the weekly calendar pages.

• "Spellcasting Basics" are included to show you how to cast a circle, ground and center, and perform a "full" spell. Further on in the book, when specific spells are described, you will need to know this information. So, if you are new to spells, please be sure to read this section.

• Write, color, and draw in this book! Take notes. Expressing your thoughts in ink is a powerful way to create your reality.

• Since this book is printed on both sides of the paper, it works best if you use colored pencils or crayons. Markers will bleed through to the other side.

• Always remember, the magic is inside you! Even if you start this book "late" in the year, or if it isn't "the best" moon phase, you are the most powerful force in your own life. You are a witch! The seasons, sun, and moon are only tools. The real magic is inside you.

Goals, Plans, and Intentions

Yes, this is a planner, but that doesn't mean you have to get intense about... planning. It's about using the powers of the universe to give you a boost, to be more "in the flow" and in tune with what you want. Work witchier, not harder! Here are some tips:

● Less is more. Go for broader feelings and intentions rather than super specific dates, processes, and outcomes. Leave room for magic to surprise you in fantastic ways.

● Make your goals big or as small as you want. Your goal or plan could be to do less.

● Instead of saying what you don't want, "to stop being an emotional wreck," phrase it positively so you feel good when you say it, "to feel at ease with my emotions."

● Any plans you make are more of a guideline. Don't be afraid to scrap them and do something else if they don't feel right anymore. It's never too late to change directions or make new plans—in fact, that's often where the best magic comes in.

Using Your Intuition

So how do you use your intuition? Follow your emotions. Emotions and intuition are woven of the same thread. Even if (especially if!) you've been called "too emotional," you can trust your emotions to be your guide. If something makes you feel "icky"— hurt, bad, anxious, nervous, hurried, chained, or dreary—stop and listen. Then figure out the message, work through it, let go of the unpleasant feelings, and restore your emotional balance by steering yourself to what feels better. Also, ask yourself, "Is this what I feel I should be doing, instead of what I want to do, or is this what someone else wants?"

Can it really be that simple? Yes. It's the key to get you going in the right direction that only YOU can feel at any moment. So what is the direction to head for? The one that makes you feel happy, excited, hopeful, or curious. The one that feels better. Go that way.

Dark, Light, and Shadow Selves

Following your good-feeling intuition doesn't mean you're "ignoring" your dark side. Just as the year has a dark half, we've all got a dark side or shadow selves—many of them. They are the unseen and often ignored parts of ourselves—self-doubt, low self-esteem, jealousy, fear, addiction, unhealthy habits, and stuckness. Whether you see shadows as obscuring the light or light as creating the shadows, this balance offers us the most powerful clues we have to our purpose and what we desire.

So... know that darkness. Use it. Acknowledge it. Know that both light and dark are essential halves of the magical seasons of your life, and the work is to walk through the shadows in order to transcend to a place of spiritual balance, purpose, and fulfillment. And, yes, this is a super-deep topic. There is so much more to explore here, so be sure to follow it if it calls you!

Wheel of the Year

IMBOLC
REST & REGENERATION
INCUBATION OF IDEAS
SACRAL CHAKRA
FEBRUARY 1, 2019

YULE
PEACE & CELEBRATION
REFLECTION & JOY
ROOT CHAKRA
DECEMBER 21, 2019
WINTER SOLSTICE

OSTARA
PLANTING SEEDS
STARTING PROJECTS
SOLAR PLEXUS CHAKRA
MARCH 20, 2019
SPRING EQUINOX

SAMHAIN
THE VEIL THINS...
SPIRITUAL CONNECTION
SOUL STAR CHAKRA
OCTOBER 31, 2019

BELTANE
GROWTH & CREATION
TAKING ACTION
HEART CHAKRA
MAY 1, 2019

Death

Rebirth

Life

MABON
LETTING GO
SECOND HARVEST
CROWN CHAKRA
SEPT. 23, 2019
AUTUMN EQUINOX

LITHA
HARNESSING
THE SUN'S POWER
THROAT CHAKRA
JUNE 21, 2019
SUMMER SOLSTICE

LUGHNASADH
FIRST HARVEST
CELEBRATION
THIRD EYE CHAKRA
AUGUST 1, 2019

Working with the Seasons & the Wheel of the Year

Think about ways you can work your life and magic in accordance with the Wheel of the Year and seasons. However, always choose what is right for you when it feels right, rather than waiting for "perfect" magical timing. Use these energies as a guideline, not as a rule. You can always start something new or let something go, no matter the season (or moon).

These cycles also remind us that there is a season of rest, reflection, and death on the opposite side of each season of growth, and that these dark times are essential parts of life.

*A Note About the Cross Quarter Dates: The dates for the two solstices and two equinoxes each year—Ostara, Litha, Mabon, and Yule—are calculated astronomically, from the position of the earth to the sun. The "cross quarter" festivals, which are the points between —Imbolc, Beltane, Lughnasadh, and Samhain—are often celebrated on "Fixed" dates instead of the actual midpoints. And so, this book lists both the "Fixed Festival Dates" (above) where it's more common to celebrate, and the "Astronomical Dates" (listed on the calendars). Choose either date or any time in between for your own festivities or ritual. 'Tis the season for magic.

The Seasons

Ostara — MARCH — Spring Equinox

Imbolc — FEBRUARY — JANUARY

Yule — DECEMBER — Winter Solstice

Samhain — NOVEMBER — OCTOBER

Mabon — SEPTEMBER — Autumnal Equinox

Lughnasadh — AUGUST — JULY

Litha — JUNE — Summer Solstice

Beltane — APRIL — MAY

LIGHT HALF - SELF EXPRESSION AND ACTUALIZATION

DARK HALF - INTROSPECTION AND REFLECTION

CELTIC DARK HALF (SAMHAIN - BELTANE)

CELTIC LIGHT HALF (BELTANE - SAMHAIN)

WINTER
Earth Element. Grounding, assessment, resting, and recalibration. Acceptance. Finding out who you are. Rebirth. Peace and total self-acceptance.

SPRING
Air Element. The mind, intellect, new beginnings, new things, new paths, passion, life-force energy of creation. Action and newness.

SUMMER
Fire Element. The sun and self. Purpose, vision, action, manifestation and abundance. Personal power and moving forward with self-confidence.

AUTUMN
Water Element. Emotions and feelings. Death. Unconscious feelings, identifying emotional patterns, reclaiming your power through feelings. Transformation. Letting go.

THE SUN IN THE ZODIAC

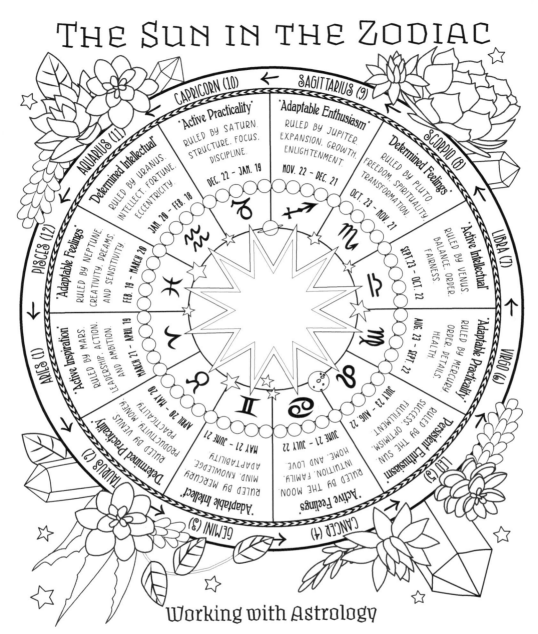

Working with Astrology

Both the moon and the sun travel through the signs of the zodiac and can wield a powerful influence on our daily lives. These cycles are different from your "natal chart," and they affect the entire population as a whole.

The moon in the signs reflects what is going on subconsciously and emotionally. The sun in the signs represents a more conscious and outwardly noticeable influence. The sun stays in each sign for about a month. The moon's cycles are much shorter, just a couple of days at most.

It's also worth noting that this kind of astrology is "electional," meaning it's used to decide when to do things, as opposed to "predictive" astrology, where you might guess at future events.

To sync up with the energy of the moon and sun's cycles, look at the weekly calendar pages to note the current sign. Then, you can use that information and the charts on these pages to help you decide when to plan things and put the astrological energy more in your favor.

The Moon in the Zodiac

Aries ♈

A physical desire to start fresh. Energy for starting and completing short-term projects. Not the best time to start long-term projects.

Taurus ♉

The sign of practical matters, the home, comfort, decor, and finances. An optimal moon sign for starting long-term projects.

Gemini ♊

A time for thinking, learning, reading, pursuing curiosities and interests, doing mental activities, and talking to fascinating people.

Cancer ♋

An auspicious time to be at home, reflect and get in touch with our feelings. Also an excellent time to focus on family and love.

Leo ♌

The sign of the self and creativity. A magical time to get in touch with your own intuition and listen for what your heart truly desires.

Virgo ♍

Organization, efficient habits, and health. The best time to start a routine or positive habit, organize, get on a schedule, or tidy things up.

Libra ♎

The sign of diplomacy, balance, and visual appeal. A good time to work on relationships, find personal balance, and hang out with friends.

Scorpio ♏

The sign of passion and desire. A good time to "find" motivation, harness your own power, take control, and rid yourself of things that no longer serve you.

Sagittarius ♐

The sign of truth and big-picture visions. This is an auspicious time to make long term plans, think big, use your imagination, and visualize a positive future.

Capricorn ♑

The sign of structure, responsibilities, and practical achievement. A time to focus on career, business and careful use of resources.

Aquarius ♒

The sign of esoterica, freethinking, and personal freedom. A good time to expand your mind to find new, unexpected ideas and solutions.

Pisces ♓

The sign of dreaming, psychic awareness, and intuition. An auspicious time for divination, reflection, mystical pursuits, and retreating into nature or water.

Void-of-Course Moon

There are void-of-course spots in between the moon signs. These are the transitionary phases, and when the moon is void of course, it can feel like a period of low energy where you may feel drained and exhausted or have trouble making decisions. Stores and businesses are "unusually" quiet, and people have trouble working together. It's also best not to start new projects or meet new people during the moon's void of course.

Often, you don't notice any difference because the void of course can be short—just a couple of minutes. But sometimes these periods can be hours or days, and that's when the shift in energy is quite noticeable! Being aware of these spots will help you use this energy to your advantage.

To see where these void spots are on the weekly calendar pages, look for the black triangles: ▶ These black triangles mark the start of the moon void-of-course cycle. The void ends when the moon enters the next sign.

Planetary Retrogrades

Retrogrades happen when the planets appear to be moving backwards in our sky. When they're going backwards, they have the opposite effect as "normal," often causing confusion or a need to "re-look" or "re-bel" or "re-treat" in their area of planetary influence. These occurances are marked on the calendar pages, as it can be helpful to be aware of their possible influences and energies.

MERCURY: Mercury rules communication, so you may experience problems with technology, messages, or conversations when it is retrograde. Back up, double check, and be extra careful with what you say and listen to. Prepare to be confused.

VENUS: Venus rules love and beauty, so be extra careful about romantic relationships, exes, and changes in your physical appearance during Venus retrograde. Don't make a drastic change in your hair and appearance or sudden decisions with love.

MARS: Mars rules power and success, so don't start something big and new when Mars is retrograde. Be extra careful and think through career or business decisions. You may feel particularly slow or unenergized.

JUPITER: Jupiter rules travel, expansion, higher education, and finances, so you may have issues with transportation, or trouble making progress when trying to expand or grow your business or career during Jupiter Retrograde. It's a good time to slow down, make sure not to overspend, and to take time to learn, study, and experiment.

SATURN: Saturn rules responsibility, structure, and discipline, and is often an influence of limitations. So when it goes retrograde, it gives an opportunity to move past failure and see beyond boundaries and comfort zones.

NEPTUNE: Neptune rules illusion, dreams, spirituality, and fantasy, so as these influences disappear during a retrograde, you may feel the stark reality of things you normally do not see. Use this time to relook at the truth versus what you've been telling yourself and find clues on how to bring dreams to reality.

URANUS: Uranus rules the unexpected, including change, liberation, and innovation. Uranus retrograde can push you to big realizations and into seeing past your limitations and fears, or show you where you need to make a change.

PLUTO: Pluto rules the shadow and the underworld. When it's retrograde, look at your shadow self and your needs for recognition, authority, and power. It's a good time to feel your own darkness and shadow and find ways to work through those things.

Spellcasting Basics

There are opening and closing steps that are basic accompaniments to spells in this book. These steps are optional but advisable: at least know "why" many witches perform these processes, and try them out for yourself.

And keep in mind, this is a super basic "coloring book" guide to the spellcasting process. There are books and online sources that go much further in-depth.

THE SECRET OF SPELLS

The secret to powerful spells is in you. Your feeling and vibration in alignment with your true source of self—or a higher power—is what makes spells work.

The secret isn't in having the right ingredients and doing all the steps in a particular order. It's in your ability to focus your intent and use your feelings, mind, and soul to call in what you want and harness the energy of the earth, plants, stars, moons, planets, and whatever other creative forces of life you like to make things happen.

BREAK THE RULES

The first rule is to throw out any of the rules that don't work for you. Do things that feel right, significant, and meaningful. Adapt spells from different practices, books, and teachers. The only way to know what works is to follow your curiosity and try things out.

USING TOOLS

Your feelings and vibration are what make the magic, not the tools, exact words, or sequences. You can cast amazing spells for free with no tools at all, and you can cast an elaborate spell that yields no results.

That said, tools like herbs, oils, crystals, and cauldrons can be powerful and fun to use in your spells. Just don't feel pressured or discouraged if you don't have much to start. Keep your magic straightforward and powerful. The right tools and ingredients will come.

"AS ABOVE, SO BELOW"

Tools, ingredients, and symbols are based on the magical theory of sympathetic magic and correspondence. You might hear the phrase, "As Above, so Below," which means the spiritual qualities of objects are passed down to earth. It's "sympathetic magic," or "this equals that," like how a totem of a lion represents that power but is not an actual lion.

Start by following lists, charts, and spells to get a feel for what others use and then begin to discover your own meaningful symbolism and correspondences.

PERMISSION

Spellbooks are like guidelines. They should be modified, simplified, or embellished to your liking. And don't degrade your magic by calling it "lazy." Keeping your witchcraft simple is okay. Go ahead, you have permission.

Also, it's not a competition to see who can use the most esoteric stuff in their spell. Hooray! It's about finding your personal power and style.

SPELLCASTING OUTLINE:

1. Plan and prepare.
2. Sage and cast a circle.
3. Ground and center.
4. Invoke a deity or connection to self.
4. Raise energy.
5. Do your spellcraft (like the spells in this book.)
6. Ground and center again.
7. Close your circle.
8. Clean up.
9. Act in accord (and be patient!).

1. PLAN AND PREPARE: If you're doing a written spell, read it several times to get familiar with it. Decide if there's anything you'll substitute or change. If you're writing your own spell (more on this later), enjoy the process and mystery of seeing the messages and theme come together.

Gather all of the items you'll be using (if any) and plan out space and time where you'll do the spell. Spells can be impromptu, so preparations can be quick and casual if you like.

2. CAST A CIRCLE AND CALL THE QUARTERS: A circle is like a container to collect the energy of your spell. Circles are also protective, with the circle of white light elevating your space and spell to the highest vibration and clearing out any negativity that might get in the way before you begin. Calling the Quarters is done to get the universal energy of the elements flowing. Sage or other incense is typically

burned at the same time to purify the air and energy. If you can't burn things, that's ok. If you've never cast a circle, try it. It's a fun, mystical experience like no other. Once you have a few candles lit and start to walk around it, magic does happen!

HOW TO CAST A CIRCLE: This is a basic, bare-bones way to cast a circle. It's often much more elaborate, and this explanation barely does it justice, so read up to find out more. And note that while some cast the circle first and then call the Quarters, some do it the other way.

1. Hold out your hand, wand, or crystal, and imagine a white light and a ball of pure energy surrounding your space, as you circle around clockwise three times. Your circle can be large or it can be tiny, just space for you and your materials.

2. Call The Four Quarters or Five Points of the Pentagram, depending on your preferences. The Quarters (also known as the Elements!) are Earth (North), Air (East), Fire (South), and Water (West). Many use the Pentagram and also call the 5th Element, Spirit or Self.

Face in each direction and say a few words to welcome the element. For example, "To the North, I call upon your power of grounding and strength. To the East, I call upon the source of knowledge. To the South, I call upon your passion and burning desire to take action. To the West, I call upon the intuition of emotion. To the spirit and source of self, I call upon your guidance and light."

3. GROUND AND CENTER: Grounding and centering prepare you to use the energy from the earth, elements, and universe. Most witches agree that if you skip these steps, you'll be drawing off of your own energy, which can be exhausting and ineffective. It's wise to ground and center both before and after a spell. It's like the difference between being "plugged in" to the magical energy of the earth and universe and "draining your batteries."

How to Ground and Center: To "ground," imagine the energy coming up from the core of the earth and into your feet, as you breathe deeply. You can visualize deep roots from your feet all the way into the center of the earth, and that these roots are pulling the earth's energy in and out of you. The point is to allow these great channels of energy to flow through you and into your spell. You can also imagine any of your negative energy, thoughts, or stress leaving.

To "center," once you've got a good flow of energy from the ground, imagine the energy shining through and out the top of your head in a pure form of you at your highest creative self, and back in as the light of guidance. Suspend yourself here between the earth and the sky, supported with the energy flowing freely through you—upheld, balanced, cleansed, and "in flow" with the energy of the universe. This process takes just a couple of minutes.

4. RAISE ENERGY: The point of raising energy is to channel the universal (magical!) forces you tapped in the previous steps to use in your spell. And raising energy is fun! You can sing, dance, chant, meditate, or do breath work. You want to do something that feels natural, so you can really get into it, lose yourself, and raise your state of consciousness.

A good way to start is to chant "Ong," allowing the roof of your mouth to vibrate ever so slightly. This vibration changes up the energy in your mind, body, and breath and is a simple yet powerful technique.

Another tip is to raise energy to the point of the "peak" where you feel it at its highest. Don't go too far where you start to tucker out or lose enthusiasm!

INVOKE A DEITY OR CREATIVE SOURCE: If you'd like to invoke a deity or your highest self to help raise energy and your vibration, call upon them. Invoking deities is way deeper than this book, so research it more if it calls to you!

5. DO YOUR SPELL: Your spell can be as simple as saying an intention and focusing on achieving the outcome of what you want, or it can be more elaborate. Whichever way you prefer, do what feels right to you.

TIPS ON VISUALIZATION AND INTENTION

Most spellwork involves a bit of visualization and intention, and here are some subtleties you can explore.

The Power of You: The most important tool in magic is you. You've got it—both power right now and vast untapped power that you can explore. To cast a successful spell, you've got to focus your mind and genuinely feel the emotions and feelings of the things you want to manifest.

If you haven't started meditating yet, start now! It's not too late, and it's easier than you think.

Visualize the Outcome

It's best to focus on the feeling of what you want, not the process of getting there. Feel the completion of your desire, and feel it powerfully.

For example, you could repeat the mantra "I have all the money I need" while feeling uneasy and worried about money in your spell, but this probably won't work. You've got to visualize and really feel the sense of calm and control you'll have when you do get the desired outcome, be it money or whatever else.

Phrase it Positively

Another tip is to phrase your intentions and desires positively. You're putting energy into this, so make sure the intention is going to be good for you. Instead of saying what you don't want, "to get out of my bad job that I hate," phrase it positively, "I want to do something that's fulfilling with my career." Then you'll be able to feel good about it, as you visualize and cast your spell.

6. GROUND AND CENTER AGAIN

After your spell, it's important to ground out any excess energy. Do this again by visualizing energy flowing through you and out. You can also imagine any "extra" energy you have petering out as you release it back into the earth.

7. CLOSE YOUR CIRCLE

If you called the Quarters or a deity, let them know the spell has ended by calling them out again.

Close your circle the opposite of as you opened it, circling around three times or more counterclockwise. Then say, "This circle is closed," or do a closing chant or song to finish your spell.

8. CLEAN UP

Don't be messy with your magic! Put away all of your spell items.

9. ACT IN ACCORD: Once you cast your spell, you've got to take action! You can cast a spell that you become a best-selling author, but if you never write a book, it's never going to happen. So you've got to take action towards what you want to open up the possibility and opportunity for it to come to you.

Look for signs, intuition, and coincidences that point you in the direction of your desires. If you get inspired after a spell, take action! Don't be surprised if you ask for money and then come up with a new idea to make money. Follow those clues, especially if they feel exciting and good.

If your spell comes true, discard and "release" any charm bag, poppet, or item you used to hold and amplify energy. Also, give thanks (if that's in your practice) or repay the universe in some way, doing something kind or of service that you feel is a solid trade for what you received from your spell.

WHAT IF YOUR SPELL DOESN'T WORK?

It's true that not all spells will work! But sometimes the results are just taking longer than you'd like, so be patient.

If your spell doesn't work, you can use divination (tarot cards and the like) or meditation to do some deeper digging into reasons why.

The good news is your own magic, power, frequency, and intention is still on your side. You can try again and add more energy in the direction of your desired outcome by casting another spell.

But give it some deep thought. What else is at play? Did you really take inspired action? Are you totally honest with yourself about what you want? Are there any thoughts or feelings about your spell or intentions that feel "off"? If so, those are clues to what you can change next time.

FOR MORE TIPS AND INSPIRATION:

Seek out websites, books, podcasts, and videos on spirituality. Follow your intuition and curiosity to deepen your practice and find your own style. And check out other books in the *Coloring Book of Shadows* series, like the *Book of Spells* and *Witch Life!*

1ST HALF 2019

January

S	M	T	W	Th	F	Sa
		1	2	3	4	5
6	7	8	9	10	11	12
13	14	15	16	17	18	19
20	21	22	23	24	25	26
27	28	29	30	31		

February

S	M	T	W	Th	F	Sa
					1	2
3	4	5	6	7	8	9
10	11	12	13	14	15	16
17	18	19	20	21	22	23
24	25	26	27	28		

March

S	M	T	W	Th	F	Sa
					1	2
3	4	5	6	7	8	9
10	11	12	13	14	15	16
17	18	19	20	21	22	23
24	25	26	27	28	29	30
31						

April

S	M	T	W	Th	F	Sa
	1	2	3	4	5	6
7	8	9	10	11	12	13
14	15	16	17	18	19	20
21	22	23	24	25	26	27
28	29	30				

May

S	M	T	W	Th	F	Sa
		1	2	3	4	
5	6	7	8	9	10	11
12	13	14	15	16	17	18
19	20	21	22	23	24	25
26	27	28	29	30	31	

June

S	M	T	W	Th	F	Sa
						1
2	3	4	5	6	7	8
9	10	11	12	13	14	15
16	17	18	19	20	21	22
23	24	25	26	27	28	29
30						

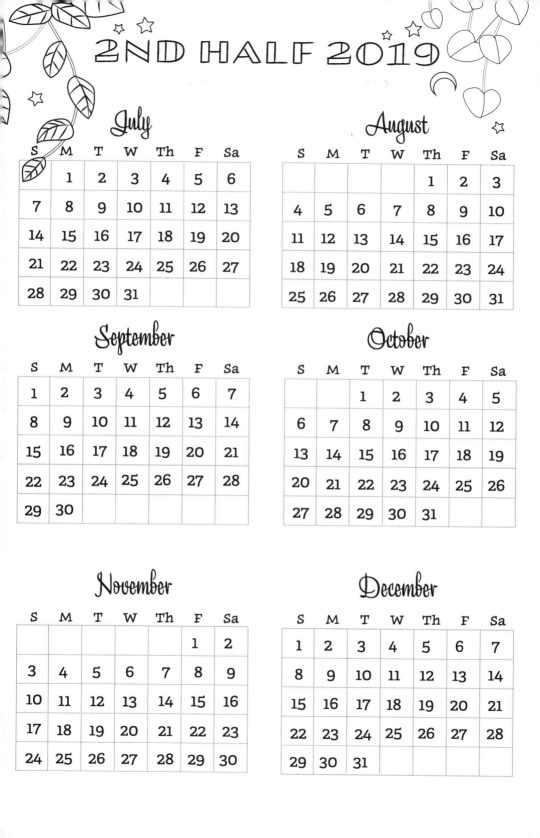

2ND HALF 2019

July

S	M	T	W	Th	F	Sa
	1	2	3	4	5	6
7	8	9	10	11	12	13
14	15	16	17	18	19	20
21	22	23	24	25	26	27
28	29	30	31			

August

S	M	T	W	Th	F	Sa
				1	2	3
4	5	6	7	8	9	10
11	12	13	14	15	16	17
18	19	20	21	22	23	24
25	26	27	28	29	30	31

September

S	M	T	W	Th	F	Sa
1	2	3	4	5	6	7
8	9	10	11	12	13	14
15	16	17	18	19	20	21
22	23	24	25	26	27	28
29	30					

October

S	M	T	W	Th	F	Sa
		1	2	3	4	5
6	7	8	9	10	11	12
13	14	15	16	17	18	19
20	21	22	23	24	25	26
27	28	29	30	31		

November

S	M	T	W	Th	F	Sa
					1	2
3	4	5	6	7	8	9
10	11	12	13	14	15	16
17	18	19	20	21	22	23
24	25	26	27	28	29	30

December

S	M	T	W	Th	F	Sa
1	2	3	4	5	6	7
8	9	10	11	12	13	14
15	16	17	18	19	20	21
22	23	24	25	26	27	28
29	30	31				

INTUITION:

REFLECTION:

VISION & INTENTION:

IMPORTANT THINGS:

GOALS:

January

Fox

Coyote

MOON ENERGY AND SPELL IDEAS

NEW & WAXING MOON: Grounding, healing, and gaining knowledge about your true self.
FULL MOON: Self-acceptance, belonging, and belief in yourself and your power.
WANING & DARK MOON: Letting go of insecurities. Banishing ill health and bad luck.

RUBY

FOLLOWING YOUR HEART

BLOODSTONE

SMOKY QUARTZ

Grounding

PHOENIX - REGENERATION

WITCH'S SELF ACCEPTANCE
A SPELL FOR EMPOWERMENT AND GROUNDING

"New Year's Resolutions" start the year off with a focus on things to change. But the seasonal energies of winter suggest it might be a wise time to accept yourself just as you are and connect to a deep, inward sense of belonging.

Things You'll Need: A dark space to sit in silence for a few moments. Optional: Three candles, black, red, and white. Earthy incense such as sandalwood, vetiver root, frankincense, yerba santa, or sage.

Cast The Spell: Light your incense. Purify the energy around you by wafting the incense smoke at your feet, then circling the smoke up and around to the top of your head, envisioning a sphere of gold or warm amber light. Feel yourself entering a safe place. If you're using candles, light them one at a time, signifying acceptance

and release of your past (black), present (red), and future (white).

Sit or lie down. Close your eyes and envision the roots of your soul shooting down into the earth. Feel yourself connecting to the part of the universe that wholly supports, loves, and cares for you just as you are. You may feel most grounded if you channel the spirit of a tree, or you may prefer to connect to an animal guide. Chant an affirmation charm such as the one below or take yourself to a meditative state as you focus on the feeling of self acceptance.

"I am a child of the elements and earth. I am accepted, I am supported, and I am enough."

When you feel a shift to a sense of universal acceptance, open your eyes and become aware of the room around you.

January 2019

	SUNDAY	MONDAY	TUESDAY
	30	31	1
	6	7	8
	13	14 ◗ First Quarter	15
	20	21 ○ Full Moon	22
	27 ◗ Last Quarter	28	29

WEDNESDAY	THURSDAY	FRIDAY	SATURDAY
2	3	4	5 ● New Moon
9	10	11	12
16	17	18	19
23	24	25	26
30	31	1	2

January 2019

MONDAY, DECEMBER 31, 2018

TUESDAY, JANUARY 1, 2019
▶ Moon void-of-course begins 5:26 PM EST

WEDNESDAY, JANUARY 2
Moon enters Sagittarius ♐ 3:58 AM EST

Stir counterclockwise to banish and release

THURSDAY, JANUARY 3

FRIDAY, JANUARY 4
▶ Moon void-of-course begins 12:41 PM EST
Moon enters Capricorn ♑ 1:54 PM EST

SATURDAY, JANUARY 5
● New Moon 8:28 PM EST

SUNDAY, JANUARY 6
⛢ Uranus goes Direct 3:27 PM

January 2019

BROCCOLI COMFORT

MONDAY, JANUARY 7
▶ Moon void-of-course begins 1:20 AM EST
Moon enters Aquarius ♒ 1:45 AM EST

TUESDAY, JANUARY 8

WEDNESDAY, JANUARY 9
▶ Moon void-of-course begins 11:52 AM EST
Moon enters Pisces ♓ 2:43 PM EST

THURSDAY, JANUARY 10

FRIDAY, JANUARY 11
▶ Moon void-of-course begins 9:24 AM EST

SATURDAY, JANUARY 12
Moon enters Aries ♈ 3:17 AM EST

SUNDAY, JANUARY 13

CARROTS, PARSNIPS, AND TURNIPS

EARTH, GROUNDING,

SALT PURIFICATION

POTATOES

January 2019

MONDAY, JANUARY 14
◑ First Quarter 1:45 AM EST
▶ Moon void-of-course begins 10:55 AM EST
Moon enters Taurus ♉ 1:31 PM EST

TUESDAY, JANUARY 15

WEDNESDAY, JANUARY 16
▶ Moon void-of-course begins 1:33 PM EST
Moon enters Gemini ♊ 8:00 PM EST

THURSDAY, JANUARY 17

FRIDAY, JANUARY 18
▶ Moon void-of-course begins 8:32 PM EST
Moon enters Cancer ♋ 10:43 PM EST

SATURDAY, JANUARY 19

SUNDAY, JANUARY 20
✿ Sun enters Aquarius ♒
▶ Moon void-of-course begins 8:49 PM EST
Moon enters Leo ♌ 10:54 PM EST

January 2019

MONDAY, JANUARY 21
○ Full Moon 12:15 AM EST

TUESDAY, JANUARY 22
▶ Moon void-of-course begins 8:19 PM EST
Moon enters Virgo ♍ 10:21 PM EST

WEDNESDAY, JANUARY 23

THURSDAY, JANUARY 24
▶ Moon void-of-course begins 8:50 AM EST
Moon enters Libra ♎ 11:02 PM EST

FRIDAY, JANUARY 25

SATURDAY, JANUARY 26

SUNDAY, JANUARY 27
▶ Moon void-of-course begins 12:20 AM EST
Moon enters Scorpio ♏ 2:30 AM EST
◑ Last Quarter 4:10 PM EST

Strength & Earth Energy

Bear

January / February 2019

MONDAY, JANUARY 28
▶ Moon void-of-course begins 5:38 PM EST

TUESDAY, JANUARY 29
Moon enters Sagittarius ♐ 9:32 AM EST

WEDNESDAY, JANUARY 30

THURSDAY, JANUARY 31
▶ Moon void-of-course begins 5:32 PM EST
Moon enters Capricorn ♑ 7:46 PM EST

FRIDAY, FEBRUARY 1
☆ IMBOLC
*Fixed Festival Date

SATURDAY, FEBRUARY 2

SUNDAY, FEBRUARY 3
▶ Moon void-of-course begins 5:52 AM EST
Moon enters Aquarius ♒ 8:02 AM EST
☼ IMBOLC
*Astronomical Date

WITCH
'N
STITCH

Mend & Heal

Spinning Wheel

- The Wheel of the Year -
Spinning the Thread of Your Dreams

INTUITION:

REFLECTION:

VISION & INTENTION:

Burn the Yule Greens

- To ward off Hobgoblins -

IMPORTANT THINGS:

Pine

GOALS:

Mistletoe

Bay

Rosemary

Out with the Old...
...In with the New

February

Poppyseed Cake

Milk

Hearty Bread & Butter

MOON ENERGY AND SPELL IDEAS

NEW & WAXING MOON: Increasing awareness of your shadow self and subconscious.
FULL MOON: Divining messages from dreams and emotions. Reawakening visions.
WANING & DARK MOON: Purification, clearing, and cleansing of emotions and space.

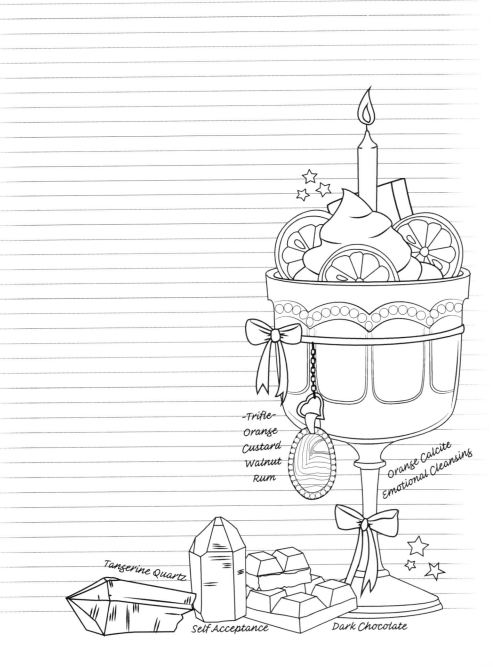

-Trifle-
Orange
Custard
Walnut
Rum

Orange Calcite
Emotional Cleansing

Tangerine Quartz

Self Acceptance

Dark Chocolate

The image above contains the text: "Have Some Tea / SO MOTE IT BE"

A SHADOWY TEA PARTY
DIVINATION WITH YOUR DARK AND LIGHT SELVES

It's important to recognize and learn from your shadow self. It gets tricky though because the shadow is subconscious or hidden, so it's difficult to see it when you're in it. Thankfully, the clarity to see the dark side is strongest in winter, so use this time to learn the secrets of your shadow. In this spell you'll invite your inner shadow self and your light self to tea. Kind of like a meeting of your inner mean girl and your inner light. Things could get interesting!

Here's What You'll Need: Tarot cards for divination. Two cups of tea: A bitter cup to represent your shadow self—wormwood, horehound, bitter melon; and a sweet cup for your light self—hibiscus, lemon, honey, or fruit. Incense, perhaps yerba santa or mugwort. A stone of truth and protection, such as obsidian,

placed between your two tea cups.

Cast the Spell: Do tarot readings for each of your selves, getting into the characters of your light and shadow. Keep it fun and lighthearted and make sure to switch teas in-between readings or messages from your two selves.

For shadow-self cards, consider their messages as things you need to work on. For light-self cards, read them as strengths and clues about your highest potential. You can pick a past, present, and future spread or ask any questions you like. Just make sure to give both sides equal time and attention!

At the end of your tea, read your tea leaves for each cup (look up "tasseography" if you've never done it before) and see what other messages you can divine for both light and shadow selves.

Brigid's Cross
Protection & Abundance

- Broom or Besom -
Purification & Cleansing
Directing Energy

Imbolc

I know I belong, I am:

(safe, secure, a child of the earth, etc.)

NORTH ▽ EARTH

The physical body, career, home, & stability.

I know I am brilliant, I believe I can:

(like a life of purpose, succeed at whatever I pursue, etc.)

EAST △ AIR

Mind, communication, & knowledge.

THE CENTER
- HIGHEST SELF -

I know my true self, and I feel

I know my emotions, I trust them to guide me towards:

(me calling in my soul, the life I want to live, etc.)

WEST ▽ WATER

Emotions, intuition, & subconscious.

SOUTH △ FIRE

Action, passion, growth, & creativity.

I know I'm empowered, I can create.

(a magical life, my own path forward, a new way, etc.)

SWEEP YOURSELF FORWARD
A BROOM SPELL AND ELEMENTAL COMPASS

Imbolc marks the midpoint of the dark half of the year, where the sun is gaining strength and you can begin to feel the seasonal shift to spring. It's an auspicious time to prepare to step into the season of light!

In this spell, you'll make an "elemental" compass to guide you into the brightest and best version of yourself. Since everyone is uniquely different, you'll get to fill in and identify your own elements, and create a personal set of affirmations that you can say or use to "sweep" yourself into the direction of your true heart, soul, and magic.

Take a few moments of meditation, or several weeks of journaling and visioning, and then fill out the above. Feel free to rewrite or change it anytime you're called. Then use these responses

as an emotional guide. What choices can you make that put you in greater alignment with the direction of your compass on a physical, mental, emotional, and spiritual level?

Your compass can also be used in a broom spell to "sweep" yourself into a higher vibration. Starting at the edge of the room and spiraling clockwise into the center, sweep your besom energetically over the floor as you chant the points of your compass. Feel yourself align with the vibration and energy of each. When you get to the center of the room, stand with your broom and feel the sense of your true direction. To finish, say, "Spiraling into the center, this is my true self, carry me forward, and so I am." Carry this energy with you, and repeat the spell if you ever feel lost or misguided.

February 2019

	SUNDAY	MONDAY	TUESDAY
	27 ◑ Last Quarter	28	29
	✿ **IMBOLC** 3 *Astronomical Date	4 ● New Moon	5
	10	11	12 ◐ First Quarter
	17	18	19 ○ Full Moon
	24	25	26 ◐ Last Quarter

Yellow, White, & Red

WEDNESDAY	THURSDAY	FRIDAY	SATURDAY
30	31	1 ☆ **IMBOLC** *Fixed Festival Date	2
6	7	8	9
13	14	15	16
20	21	22	23
27	28	1	2

February 2019

Search for fallen branches to craft wands, staffs, and besom handles

MONDAY, FEBRUARY 4
● New Moon 4:03PM EST

TUESDAY, FEBRUARY 5
▶ Moon void-of-course begins 6:58 PM EST
Moon enters Pisces ♓ 9:01 PM EST

WEDNESDAY, FEBRUARY 6

THURSDAY, FEBRUARY 7
▶ Moon void-of-course begins 5:13 PM EST

FRIDAY, FEBRUARY 8
Moon enters Aries ♈ 9:33 AM EST

SATURDAY, FEBRUARY 9

SUNDAY, FEBRUARY 10
▶ Moon void-of-course begins 6:47 PM EST
Moon enters Taurus ♉ 8:28 PM EST

Rowan - Magic and Protection

Hazel - Wisdom and Luck

Birch - Protection and Purification

February 2019

– Primrose –
Love, Protection, & Health

MONDAY, FEBRUARY 11

TUESDAY, FEBRUARY 12
◑ First Quarter 5:26 PM EST
▶ Moon void-of-course begins 5:26 PM EST

WEDNESDAY, FEBRUARY 13
Moon enters Gemini ♊ 4:31 AM EST

THURSDAY, FEBRUARY 14

FRIDAY, FEBRUARY 15
▶ Moon void-of-course begins 7:48 AM EST
Moon enters Cancer ♋ 9:02 AM EST

SATURDAY, FEBRUARY 16

Lamb – Innocence & New Life

SUNDAY, FEBRUARY 17
▶ Moon void-of-course begins 9:17 AM EST
Moon enters Leo ♌ 10:20 AM EST

February 2019

MONDAY, FEBRUARY 18

TUESDAY, FEBRUARY 19
✿ Sun enters Pisces ♓
▶ Moon void-of-course begins 8:50 AM EST
Moon enters Virgo ♍ 9:46 AM EST
◯ Full Moon 10:53 AM EST

WEDNESDAY, FEBRUARY 20
▶ Moon void-of-course begins 8:51 PM EST

THURSDAY, FEBRUARY 21
Moon enters Libra ♎ 9:17 AM EST

FRIDAY, FEBRUARY 22

SATURDAY, FEBRUARY 23
▶ Moon void-of-course begins 10:10 AM EST
Moon enters Scorpio ♏ 10:55 AM EST

SUNDAY, FEBRUARY 24

Leeks

Basil

Rosemary

Sage

February/March 2019

MONDAY, FEBRUARY 25
▶ Moon void-of-course begins 7:13 AM EST
Moon enters Sagittarius ♐ 4:19 PM EST

TUESDAY, FEBRUARY 26
◑ Last Quarter 6:26 AM EST

WEDNESDAY, FEBRUARY 27

THURSDAY, FEBRUARY 28
▶ Moon void-of-course begins 1:17 AM EST
Moon enters Capricorn ♑ 1:47 AM EST

FRIDAY, MARCH 1

SATURDAY, MARCH 2
▶ Moon void-of-course begins 1:47 PM EST
Moon enters Aquarius ♒ 2:06 PM EST

SUNDAY, MARCH 3

- Duck -
Comfort & Happiness
Adapting with the Seasons

INTUITION:

REFLECTION:

VISION & INTENTION:

IMPORTANT THINGS:

GOALS:

Pastel Yellow, Green & Pink

- Clover -
Three Leaves - Protection
Four Leaves - Luck

March

Unicorn - Dreams

Eggs - New Life, Fertility, & Abundance

Waffles

Hot Cross Buns
4 Quarters of the Moon

MOON ENERGY AND SPELL IDEAS

NEW & WAXING MOON: Growing things, starting new projects, and planning for success.
FULL MOON: Setting intentions and visualizing the outcome, taking action, making change.
WANING & DARK MOON: Banishing anxiety or cynicism about change and starting new things.

Rose – Happiness

Mugwort
-and-
Calendula

Visions

Clear Quartz – Clarity of Self

THE BEST WITCH

A BATH SPELL TO VISUALIZE YOUR MOST MAGICAL SELF

Sometimes you have to get out of your own way to allow space for your intuition to be heard. The bath (or shower) is a powerful place to succumb to the element of water and your subconscious. It's a magical place for idea generation because it allows you to relax and let your true brilliance and guidance shine.

While you run your bath, light some candles and empowering incense, such as cinquefoil, frankincense, or bay. Place crystals like clear quartz or amethyst (to amplify your sense of self) and citrine (happiness) on the edges or in the water. Dump in 1/2 cup of salt and 1/4 cup of herbs for positive visions such as mugwort, rose, calendula, jasmine, and lemon. Hold the intention to clear the static and shadow, and allow your highest and best nature, new ideas,

and best self to rise. If you are taking a shower, mix the salt and herbs with 1/2 cup of jojoba oil or shea butter to make a body scrub.

Get in the bath. As you're fully immersed in water, allow yourself to visualize your best self. Feel yourself as happy, successful, and fulfilled, abundant, or as peaceful as you want, in whatever ways that feel right. Then relax and let your mind empty of all thoughts and visions, allowing silence or subconscious energy to arise and fill you with inspiration, new ideas, and a "next" level of yourself, your consciousness, and what you desire.

After your spell and for the next several days, take notes of any ideas or visions that came to you, and use them to guide your Ostara intentions for the year in the next spell.

Fire Opal

Reawakening your power

Spring Equinox Rain

Collect and use in spells to start new things or add energy for growth.

Ostara

INTENTION-SETTING RITUAL
PLANT THE SEEDS FOR YOUR MAGICAL YEAR

Ostara or the Spring Equinox holds the most powerful seasonal energy to start new projects and phases in life. At the minimum, do the visioning portion of this spell every year. If you want to get crafty, make a terrarium, or plant real seeds in dirt if you've got a green thumb.

1. THINK: A few weeks before the Equinox, do the previous bath spell or think of 1-3 things you want to manifest this year. Write them down. Make them clear, specific, and positive. Focus on the feeling that you want to bring to life.

2. PREPARE: Look up the exact day and time of the Spring Equinox for your time zone. Plan to have at least 30 minutes.

3. FOR EACH MANIFESTATION:

- VISUALIZE: See and feel what you'd like through your third eye. Immerse yourself in the feeling of already having it in the present.

- MEDITATE: To deepen the feeling.

- VISUALIZE AGAIN: Bring your visualization the lower back of your head, and reflect on it again. If your neck gets tingly—awesome!

- Say "And so it shall be!" or "It is done."

4. REPEAT STEP 3 for each manifestation.

5. CLOSE: Take a few minutes to lock in all the positive feelings and intentions at the end.

6. TAKE ACTION: Let go of expectations and act in accord by taking inspired action.

If you'd like to make a terrarium to enhance your spell's energy, fill a small jar or earthen vessel with quartz pebbles (rose quartz, if you want to manifest love!) and any other meaningful accents of your choice: larger crystals, deity statues, notes, photographs, or herbs. Hold your crystal terrarium during the spell, then place it on your altar. Recharge it as the year progresses by placing it under the full moon's light.

March 2019

	SUNDAY	MONDAY	TUESDAY
	24	25	26 ◑ Last Quarter
	3	4	5
	10	11	12
	17	18	19
	24	25	26
	31	1	2

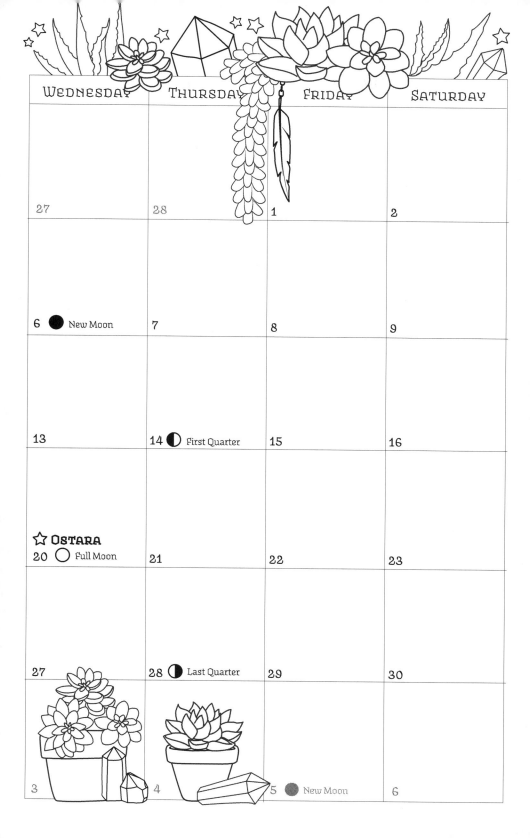

WEDNESDAY	THURSDAY	FRIDAY	SATURDAY
27	28	1	2
6 ● New Moon	7	8	9
13	14 ◐ First Quarter	15	16
☆ **OSTARA** 20 ○ Full Moon	21	22	23
27	28 ◐ Last Quarter	29	30
3	4	5 ● New Moon	6

March 2019

MONDAY, MARCH 4

TUESDAY, MARCH 5
▶ Moon void-of-course begins 3:05 AM EST
Moon enters Pisces ♓ 3:10 AM EST
☿℞ Mercury Retrograde 1:19 PM - 3/28/19

WEDNESDAY, MARCH 6
● New Moon 11:03 AM EST

THURSDAY, MARCH 7
▶ Moon void-of-course begins 2:08 PM EST
Moon enters Aries ♈ 3:27 PM EST

FRIDAY, MARCH 8

SATURDAY, MARCH 9
▶ Moon void-of-course begins 12:13 PM EST

SUNDAY, MARCH 10
Moon enters Taurus ♉ 3:09 AM EST

Orange Selenite Brings Dreams to Reality

Dandelion Makes Wishes Come True

FUTURE Success

Ask: How can I grow into the most magical version of myself?

March 2019

MONDAY, MARCH 11

TUESDAY, MARCH 12
▶ Moon void-of-course begins 5:30 AM EST
Moon enters Gemini ♊ 11:47 AM EST

WEDNESDAY, MARCH 13

THURSDAY, MARCH 14
◐ First Quarter 6:26 AM EST
▶ Moon void-of-course begins 8:30 AM EST
Moon enters Cancer ♋ 5:29 PM EST

FRIDAY, MARCH 15

SATURDAY, MARCH 16
▶ Moon void-of-course begins 2:02 PM EST
Moon enters Leo ♌ 8:56 PM EST

SUNDAY, MARCH 17

Transformation

snake

March 2019

MONDAY, MARCH 18
▶ Moon void-of-course begins 11:18 AM EST
Moon enters Virgo ♍ 9:41 PM EST

TUESDAY, MARCH 19

WEDNESDAY, MARCH 20
▶ Moon void-of-course begins 11:21 AM EST
Moon enters Libra ♎ 9:27 PM EST
◯ Full Moon 9:42 PM EST
☆ **Ostara - Spring Equinox**

THURSDAY, MARCH 21
✹ Sun enters Aries ♈

FRIDAY, MARCH 22
▶ Moon void-of-course begins 2:10 PM EST
Moon enters Scorpio ♏ 10:16 PM EST

SATURDAY, MARCH 23

SUNDAY, MARCH 24
▶ Moon void-of-course begins 10:23 PM EST

Cat's Eye - Energy & Focus for Success

March 2019

MONDAY, MARCH 25
Moon enters Sagittarius ♐ 2:05 AM EST

TUESDAY, MARCH 26
▶ Moon void-of-course begins 10:36 PM EST

WEDNESDAY, MARCH 27
Moon enters Capricorn ♑ 10:07 AM EST

THURSDAY, MARCH 28
◐ Last Quarter 12:09 AM EST
☿ Mercury goes Direct 9:59 AM

FRIDAY, MARCH 29
▶ Moon void-of-course begins 8:04 PM EST
Moon enters Aquarius ♒ 9:45 PM EST

SATURDAY, MARCH 30

SUNDAY, MARCH 31
▶ Moon void-of-course begins 11:01 PM EST

Asparagus
Power & Vigor

Carrot & Hare
Fertility, Action, & Life

INTUITION:

REFLECTION:

VISION & INTENTION:

IMPORTANT THINGS:

GOALS:

Chocolate - Love & Wealth

Braided Egg Bread - The endless cycle of seasons

April

Tulips
Love & Prosperity

Chocolate Bunnies

Chick - New Life

Jelly Egg

MOON ENERGY AND SPELL IDEAS

NEW & WAXING MOON: Starting new projects, taking action, and following your curiosity.
FULL MOON: Energy, strength, growth, happiness, and resurrection of your true self.
WANING & DARK MOON: Reflecting on self-doubt and inaction, then banishing any issues.

Daffodil

Love & Luck

Yellow Topaz

Shining a Light Forward & Directing Energy

Elemental Action
Move Forward And Create Positive Change

In early spring, the turn of the seasons is unmistakable as the energy shifts to growth and new life. You can use this energy to create momentum with inspired action for your Ostara intentions or other spells and rituals.

At the first new moon after the Spring Equinox, or at any other new moon, start journaling, thinking, divining, and looking through these five "elemental lenses" as a guide for your thoughts, questions, research, and action. You can focus on one per day, or you can reflect on a little bit of each as you feel called.

Take action and follow your intuition when you come up with exciting new ideas. Then keep rotating through all five of the lenses, putting pieces together as you go, paying special attention to any coincidences, clues, intuitive flashes, good feelings, or patterns that arise.

You might also want to try working with "Air" and "Fire" elements during the waxing moon phase, "Spirit" at the full moon, and "Water" and "Earth" during the waning moon phase.

Earth: What is my purpose and vision? What would I need to do to make my dreams real?

Air: What else do I need to learn? What's missing? How can I be more open to new information and insights?

Fire: How can I take action? How can I move things forward? What do I need to do to change, harness, or rebalance my energy?

Water: What feelings have I been avoiding? How can I use my emotions as guidance?

Spirit: How can I act in accord with what is true to my heart and soul's purpose?

April 2019

	Sunday	Monday	Tuesday
	31	1	2
	7	8	9
	14	15	16
	21	22	23
	28	29	30

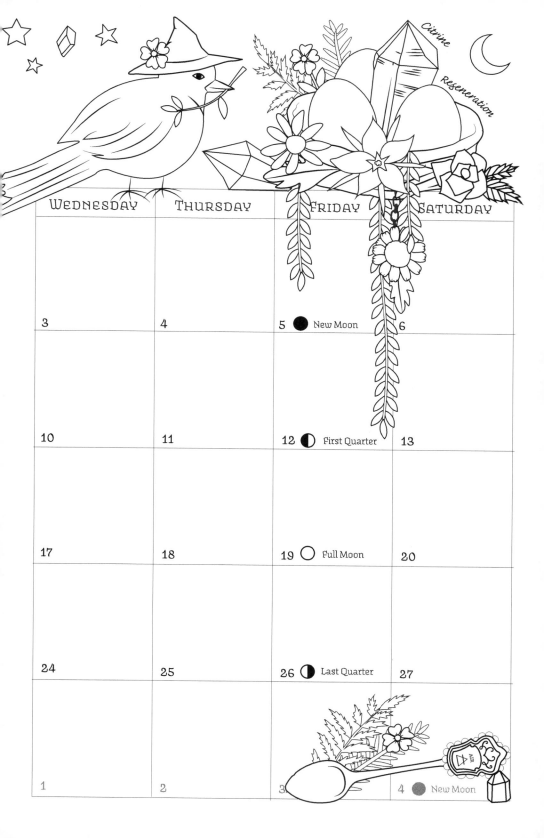

Citrine

Reseneration

WEDNESDAY	THURSDAY	FRIDAY	SATURDAY
3	4	5 ● New Moon	6
10	11	12 ◑ First Quarter	13
17	18	19 ○ Full Moon	20
24	25	26 ◑ Last Quarter	27
1	2	3	4 ● New Moon

April 2019

MONDAY, APRIL 1
Moon enters Pisces ♓ 10:47 AM EST

TUESDAY, APRIL 2

WEDNESDAY, APRIL 3
▶ Moon void-of-course begins 11:35 AM EST
Moon enters Aries ♈ 10:56 PM EST

THURSDAY, APRIL 4

FRIDAY, APRIL 5
● New Moon 4:50 AM EST
▶ Moon void-of-course begins 10:14 PM EST

SATURDAY, APRIL 6
Moon enters Taurus ♉ 9:06 AM EST

SUNDAY, APRIL 7

Violet

Yellow

Sea Foam Green

April 2019

MONDAY, APRIL 8
▶ Moon void-of-course begins 4:28 AM EST
Moon enters Gemini ♊ 5:14 PM EST

TUESDAY, APRIL 9

WEDNESDAY, APRIL 10
♃ Jupiter Retrograde 1:01 PM - 8/11/19
▶ Moon void-of-course begins 1:26 PM EST
Moon enters Cancer ♋ 11:31 PM EST

THURSDAY, APRIL 11

FRIDAY, APRIL 12
◑ First Quarter 3:05 PM EST
▶ Moon void-of-course begins 7:32 PM EST

SATURDAY, APRIL 13
Moon enters Leo ♌ 3:50 AM EST

SUNDAY, APRIL 14
▶ Moon void-of-course begins 9:38 PM EST

Transforming Energy into Power

Amber

Passion & Womanhood

Azalea

April 2019

MONDAY, APRIL 15
Moon enters Virgo ♍ 6:13 AM EST

TUESDAY, APRIL 16

WEDNESDAY, APRIL 17
▶ Moon void-of-course begins 12:29 AM EST
Moon enters Libra ♎ 7:21 AM EST

THURSDAY, APRIL 18

FRIDAY, APRIL 19
◯ Full Moon 7:12 AM EST
▶ Moon void-of-course begins 7:12 AM EST
Moon enters Scorpio ♏ 8:40 AM EST

SATURDAY, APRIL 20
▶ Moon void-of-course begins 11:59 PM EST
✿ Sun enters Taurus ♉

SUNDAY, APRIL 21
Moon enters Sagittarius ♐ 11:59 AM EST

April 2019

MONDAY, APRIL 22

TUESDAY, APRIL 23
▶ Moon void-of-course begins 7:43 AM EST
Moon enters Capricorn ♑ 6:49 PM EST

WEDNESDAY, APRIL 24
♇℞ Pluto Retrograde 2:48 PM - 10/03/19

THURSDAY, APRIL 25
▶ Moon void-of-course begins 3:47 PM EST

FRIDAY, APRIL 26
Moon enters Aquarius ♒ 5:27 AM EST
◐ Last Quarter 6:18 PM EST

SATURDAY, APRIL 27

SUNDAY, APRIL 28
▶ Moon void-of-course begins 5:43 AM EST
Moon enters Pisces ♓ 6:11 PM EST

Lilac - Spirituality

April/May 2019

MONDAY, APRIL 29
♄℞ Saturn Retrograde 8:54 PM - 9/18/19

TUESDAY, APRIL 30
▶ Moon void-of-course begins 5:57 PM EST

WEDNESDAY, MAY 1
Moon enters Aries ♈ 6:23 AM EST
☆ Beltane
*Fixed Festival Date

THURSDAY, MAY 2

FRIDAY, MAY 3
▶ Moon void-of-course begins 4:47 AM EST
Moon enters Taurus ♉ 4:17 PM EST

SATURDAY, MAY 4
● New Moon 6:45 PM EST

SUNDAY, MAY 5
▶ Moon void-of-course begins 11:10 AM EST
Moon enters Gemini ♊ 11:39 PM EST
☆ Beltane
*Astronomical Date

Sweet Woodruff
Prosperity and Success

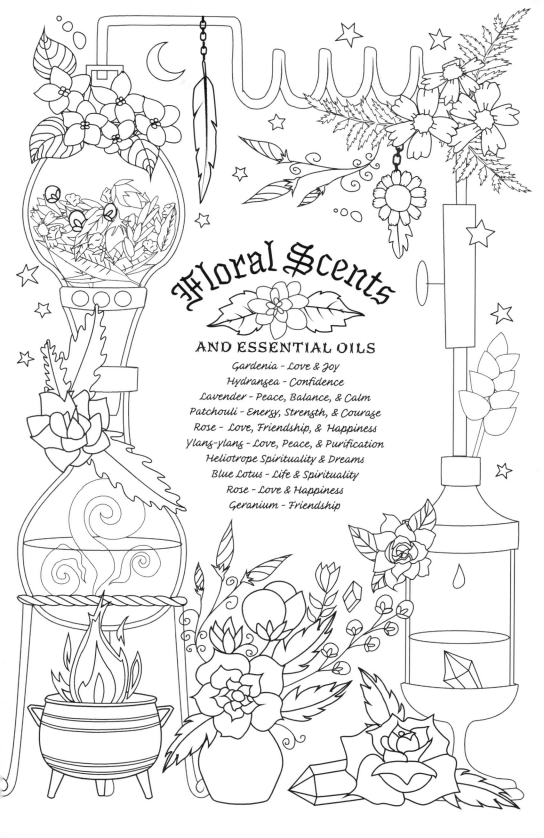

Floral Scents

AND ESSENTIAL OILS

Gardenia – Love & Joy
Hydrangea – Confidence
Lavender – Peace, Balance, & Calm
Patchouli – Energy, Strength, & Courage
Rose – Love, Friendship, & Happiness
Ylang-ylang – Love, Peace, & Purification
Heliotrope Spirituality & Dreams
Blue Lotus – Life & Spirituality
Rose – Love & Happiness
Geranium – Friendship

INTUITION:

REFLECTION:

VISION & INTENTION:

IMPORTANT THINGS:

GOALS:

May

HAWTHORN
"MAY BLOSSOMS"
FAERIE MAGIC

MOON ENERGY AND SPELL IDEAS

NEW & WAXING MOON: Attracting love, passion, abundance, and increasing your vitality.
FULL MOON: Igniting your power, bringing your dreams to life, cultivating your spirituality.
WANING & DARK MOON: Banishing fears and releasing resentment towards those you love.

Rose - Love

Violets - Friendship

The Green Man & Goddess Flora
An Offering to the Green Spirits of Nature

Observing the beauty and power of nature connects you to the magic of the earth. You can see and feel the seasons changing. They are "living" proof of the sacred balance of dark and light and the spiral of life where all things live, die, and cycle through as part of the universal energy of creation.

If you've ever felt the spirit of a tree, plant, or forest—you've been in the presence of the Green Man. He represents the spirit of plants and transcends thousands of years of natural magic. The Goddess Flora is a deity and personification of the magic of flowers, celebrated with perfume, garlands, floral bouquets, and symbols of love, pleasure, fertility, and new life.

To make an offering to one of these green spirits, plan to spend some time outside with nature. Think about and be grateful for all of the abundance that the earth offers you. Then, consider what you can give back and make an "offering" in exchange (to be kinder, smile more, raise your vibration, donate time or resources, make people laugh, etc.).

You can also give back in a symbolic way by "offering libations." Bring a flask of wine or floral tea with you as you spend time in nature. Drink half, and pour half to the earth as an offering to the green spirits.

Flowers and greenery can add extra magic and beauty to your altar, home, and spellwork. Try casting a circle with leaves and petals, or create a mandala from rocks, sticks, and flowers. Use botanical scents and essential oils to enhance the energy of your spellwork and daily rituals.

Beltane

A Celebration of Fire
Connecting to the Powers of Life and Magic

Beltane is a festival of passion and life, traditionally celebrated with a bonfire. Cattle were run between bale fires to bless and protect them, and people jumped over flames to cast wishes. If you're able to light a bonfire—by all means, do! But if that's not in the cards, you can light a ritual fire with a candle or small cauldron.

Things You'll Need: Anoint a candle with cinnamon, clove, or olive oil. Then roll the candle in a mixture of basil, bay, and cedar to signify money, strength, and protection, or any combination and intention of herbs you desire. Keep extra herbs on hand to fling and cast as wishes during your ritual.

For a cauldron with a blue Strega "spirit flame," place several spoonfuls of dried herbs (above) into your cauldron and pour a shot of 181 tequila or another high-proof alcohol on top. Procure a long-handled lighter or wooden matches to light it with. And NEVER pour alcohol into a fire straight from the bottle—put it in a glass first. Always keep an extinguisher on hand and practice *extreme* fire safety.

Performing The Ritual: Cast a circle of petals and herbs around your unlit candle, cauldron, or bonfire. Set an intention to stoke your personal fire and passions, then light the flame.

In a traditional "jumping the fire" ritual, you make a wish as you jump over the balefire. For these lower-key flames, cast your wish or intention as you toss herbs into the flaming cauldron or sprinkle herbs clockwise around your candle. Then dance, chant, sing, play— or whatever makes you feel alive and passionate!

May 2019

	SUNDAY	MONDAY	TUESDAY
	28	29	30
	☼ BELTANE 5 *Astronomical Date	6	7
	12	13	14
	19	20	21
	26 ◐ Last Quarter	27	28

Green & Pink

WEDNESDAY	THURSDAY	FRIDAY	SATURDAY
☆ **BELTANE** 1 *Fixed Festival Date	2	3	4 ● New Moon
8	9	10	11 ◗ First Quarter
15	16	17	18 ○ Full Moon
22	23	24	25
29	30	31	

May 2019

- Hydransea -
Confidence

MONDAY, MAY 6

TUESDAY, MAY 7
▶ Moon void-of-course begins 7:49 PM EST

WEDNESDAY, MAY 8
Moon enters Cancer ♋ 5:06 AM EST

THURSDAY, MAY 9
▶ Moon void-of-course begins 10:05 PM EST

FRIDAY, MAY 10
Moon enters Leo ♌ 9:13 AM EST

SATURDAY, MAY 11
◑ First Quarter 9:12 PM EST

SUNDAY, MAY 12
▶ Moon void-of-course begins 8:24 AM EST
Moon enters Virgo ♍ 12:21 PM EST

Pink Tourmaline
Compassion, Love, & Self-Love

Emerald
Inspiration, Love, & Balance

May 2019

Invite faeries to your garden on the Full Moon in May

MONDAY, MAY 13

TUESDAY, MAY 14
▶ Moon void-of-course begins 1:18 PM EST
Moon enters Libra ♎ 2:50PM EST

WEDNESDAY, MAY 15

THURSDAY, MAY 16
▶ Moon void-of-course begins 5:37 AM EST
Moon enters Scorpio ♏ 5:25 AM EST

FRIDAY, MAY 17

SATURDAY, MAY 18
○ Full Moon 5:11 PM EST
▶ Moon void-of-course begins 5:11 PM EST
Moon enters Sagittarius ♐ 9:20 PM EST

SUNDAY, MAY 19

Green Calcite
Positive Mental Balance

Rose Quartz

Love & Peace

May 2019

MONDAY, MAY 20
▶ Moon void-of-course begins 1:04 PM EST

TUESDAY, MAY 21
Moon enters Capricorn ♑ 3:56 AM EST
✿ Sun enters Gemini ♊

Daisy - Friendship

WEDNESDAY, MAY 22
▶ Moon void-of-course begins 11:57 PM EST

THURSDAY, MAY 23
Moon enters Aquarius ♒ 1:49 PM EST

FRIDAY, MAY 24

Cat - Magic

SATURDAY, MAY 25
▶ Moon void-of-course begins 8:50 AM EST

SUNDAY, MAY 26
Moon enters Pisces ♓ 2:07 AM EST
◐ Last Quarter 12:33 PM EST

Jade *Harmony*

May/June 2019

MONDAY, MAY 27

TUESDAY, MAY 28
▶ Moon void-of-course begins 12:20 AM EST
Moon enters Aries ♈ 2:31 PM EST

WEDNESDAY, MAY 29

THURSDAY, MAY 30
▶ Moon void-of-course begins 11:07 AM EST

FRIDAY, MAY 31
Moon enters Taurus ♉ 12:42 AM EST

SATURDAY, JUNE 1
▶ Moon void-of-course begins 6:52 PM EST

SUNDAY, JUNE 2
Moon enters Gemini ♊ 7:47 AM EST

Elder Wand - Protection & Magic

Pansy - Love & Happiness

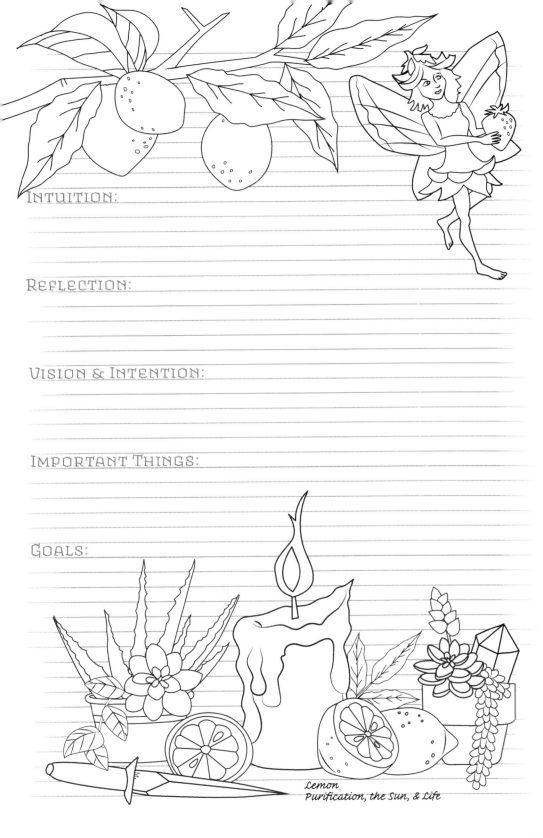

Intuition:

Reflection:

Vision & Intention:

Important Things:

Goals:

Lemon
Purification, the Sun, & Life

June

MOON ENERGY AND SPELL IDEAS

NEW & WAXING MOON: Increasing confidence, abundance, and making new friends.
FULL MOON: Protection, celebrating your success, and divination for your highest self.
WANING & DARK MOON: Releasing self-doubt, perfectionism, and negative emotions.

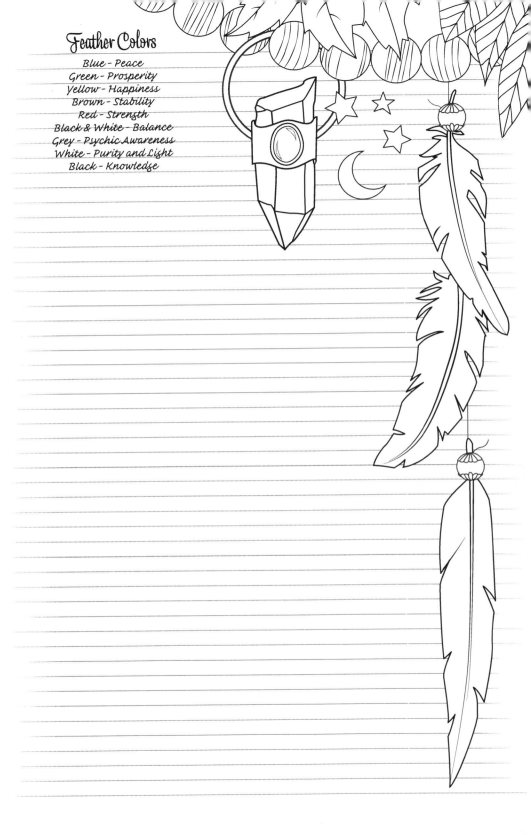

Feather Colors

Blue - Peace
Green - Prosperity
Yellow - Happiness
Brown - Stability
Red - Strength
Black & White - Balance
Grey - Psychic Awareness
White - Purity and Light
Black - Knowledge

WITCH'S LADDER

A CHARM FOR PROTECTION OR OTHER WORKINGS

Midsummer, or Litha, marks the longest day of the year and is the celebration of the sun's full strength. The sun symbolizes the light and life of a higher power, the light within yourself, and an elevated realm of consciousness.

Crafting a charm of protection and strength is a classic activity among witches. You can also work intentions of abundance, life, fertility, love, wishes, or anything else you want to power up with the sun's sacred light.

Make a traditional Witch's Ladder by braiding three 3-foot strands of yarn (red, white, and black). Then sew an odd number of feathers in symbolic colors, evenly spaced, along the length of the braid. Tie the ends of the braid together so it forms a circle. Feel free to chant a rhyme or a witchy poem while you braid and sew, and keep your intention in your mind as you craft it.

If you want to get fancier and more creative, you can use different colors of yarn and feathers, or add beads, charms, sprigs of herbs, or other symbolic embellishments for your intentions.

Create your charm a few weeks before the solstice. At noon on the solstice day, perform this simple spell with your witch's ladder to enchant it with the power of the sun.

Place your charm outside at noon. Sprinkle salt on it to purify, then say your intentions for protection, strength, abundance, or whatever you've chosen. Keep your charm outside for at least three hours or until sundown. If you are lighting a bonfire or candle spell at sundown, you can also pass your charm over the ritual flame to enhance the power of the spell.

Yarrow
Courage & Psychic Powers

Honey Cakes - Sunny Happiness
Bees - Productivity & Nature's Sweetness

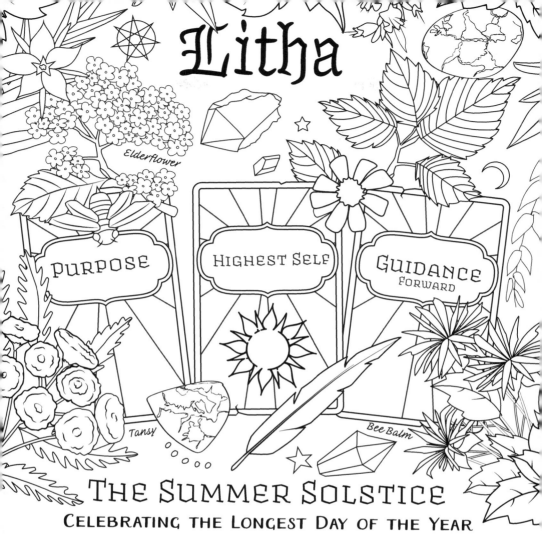

Litha

Elderflower

PURPOSE

HIGHEST SELF

GUIDANCE
FORWARD

Tansy

Bee Balm

THE SUMMER SOLSTICE
CELEBRATING THE LONGEST DAY OF THE YEAR

The sun reaches its highest point and power at noon on the summer solstice, marking a powerful shift from light to dark. It's an "in-between" time, a chance to slip into another world and change the course of your future. The sun represents the self. This is a time where you can see and connect clearly with your own true "you" and personal power.

It's a magical day, so why not experience the longest day of the year at its fullest —from dawn to noon to sundown?

At Sunrise: In ancient times, various cultures built temples to catch the first rays of sun on the summer solstice—like Stonehenge. Familiarize yourself with when and where the first rays of sun will hit your yard or other outdoor location.

As the first ray of sun arrives, ring bells, yell, chant, sing, and welcome the light. Or do a meditation with your eyes closed where you get in touch with your inner light as you feel the sun's first rays.

At Noon: Make a positive choice or a change for yourself. If something has been holding you back or feeling "wrong," cast a spell and declare that you are going to make a change for the better. The doors to any other life or situation you desire are open. Take this opportunity to walk through.

At Sunset: Do some divination! Set up a candlelit tarot table—outside at sunset if you can. Get a cup of honey whiskey or tea with lemon and honey—and pull some tarot cards. Ask questions to guide you towards the fulfillment of your highest self and purpose.

June 2019

SUNDAY	MONDAY	TUESDAY
26 ◖ Last Quarter	27	28
2	3 ● New Moon	4
9	10 ◑ First Quarter	11
16	17 ○ Full Moon	18
23	24	25 ◑ Last Quarter
30	1	2 ● New Moon

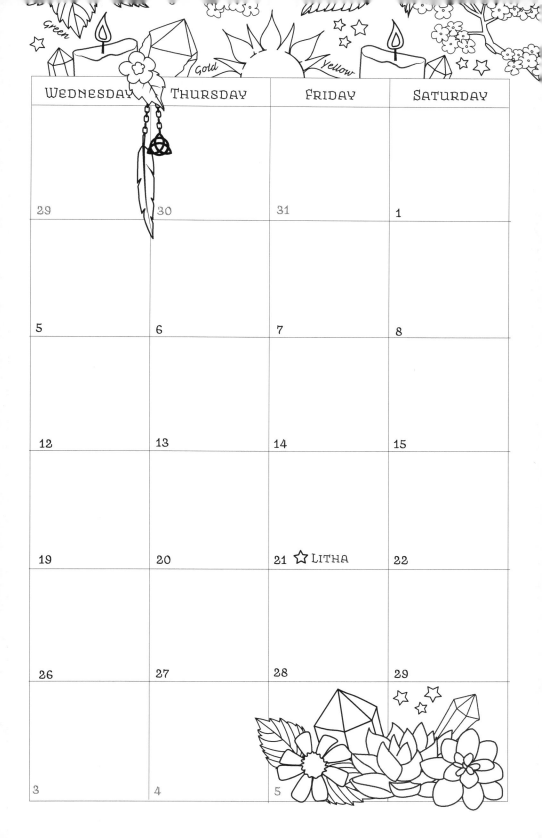

WEDNESDAY	THURSDAY	FRIDAY	SATURDAY
29	30	31	1
5	6	7	8
12	13	14	15
19	20	21 ☆ LITHA	22
26	27	28	29
3	4	5	

Green   Gold   Yellow

June 2019

MONDAY, JUNE 3
● New Moon 6:01 AM EST

TUESDAY, JUNE 4
▶ Moon void-of-course begins 11:41 AM EST
Moon enters Cancer ♋ 12:16 PM EST

WEDNESDAY, JUNE 5

THURSDAY, JUNE 6
▶ Moon void-of-course begins 10:10 AM EST
Moon enters Leo ♌ 3:15 PM EST

FRIDAY, JUNE 7

SATURDAY, JUNE 8
▶ Moon void-of-course begins 5:23 PM EST
Moon enters Virgo ♍ 5:44 PM EST

SUNDAY, JUNE 9

Caterpillar
Patience & Diligence

June 2019

MONDAY, JUNE 10

◑ First Quarter 1:59 AM EST
▶ Moon void-of-course begins 8:01 AM EST
Moon enters Libra ♎ 8:28 PM EST

TUESDAY, JUNE 11

WEDNESDAY, JUNE 12

▶ Moon void-of-course begins 11:15 AM EST

THURSDAY, JUNE 13

Moon enters Scorpio ♏ 12:02 AM EST

FRIDAY, JUNE 14

▶ Moon void-of-course begins 3:45 PM EST

SATURDAY, JUNE 15

Moon enters Sagittarius ♐ 5:02 AM EST

SUNDAY, JUNE 16

Turquoise

Expression of Self

June 2019

MONDAY, JUNE 17
○ Full Moon 4:30 AM EST
▶ Moon void-of-course begins 4:30 AM EST
Moon enters Capricorn ♑ 12:13 PM EST

TUESDAY, JUNE 18

WEDNESDAY, JUNE 19
▶ Moon void-of-course begins 7:18 AM EST
Moon enters Aquarius ♒ 10:00 PM EST

THURSDAY, JUNE 20

FRIDAY, JUNE 21
▶ Moon void-of-course begins 10:01 AM EST
✿ Sun enters Cancer ♋
♆℞ Neptune Retrograde 10:36 AM - 11/27/2019
☆ LITHA - SUMMER SOLSTICE

SATURDAY, JUNE 22
Moon enters Pisces ♓ 10:01 AM EST

SUNDAY, JUNE 23

Drink mead or honey tea under the full moon in June

Honey - Happiness of Life Health & Healing

June 2019

Moonstone
Intuition and Psychic Abilities

MONDAY, JUNE 24
▶ Moon void-of-course begins 7:10 PM EST
Moon enters Aries ♈ 10:37 PM EST

TUESDAY, JUNE 25
◑ Last Quarter 5:46 AM EST

WEDNESDAY, JUNE 26

THURSDAY, JUNE 27
▶ Moon void-of-course begins 3:51 AM EST
Moon enters Taurus ♉ 9:31 AM EST

FRIDAY, JUNE 28

SATURDAY, JUNE 29
▶ Moon void-of-course begins 2:38 PM EST
Moon enters Gemini ♊ 5:08 PM EST

SUNDAY, JUNE 30

Cinquefoil - Happiness & Magic

INTUITION: _____

REFLECTION: _____

VISION & INTENTION: _____

IMPORTANT THINGS: _____

GOALS: _____

Lake Sand
Tranquility & Awareness

Ocean Sand

Change, Transformation, & Healing

River Sand
Action & Change

July

Pelican - Abundance

MOON ENERGY AND SPELL IDEAS

NEW & WAXING MOON: Increasing confidence in your voice, vision, and creative expression.
FULL MOON: Divination for your highest self and discovering your true purpose.
WANING & DARK MOON: Releasing emotional patterns that are holding back your true self.

Lavender

Chamomile

Rose Hips

CREATIVI-TEA

INVOKE YOUR CREATIVITY AND SELF EXPRESSION

In July, the sun signs of Cancer (emotions) and Leo (self) lend their influences to seasonal energy that's already fueled by expressive solar power. It's a magical time to "create" or express yourself by journaling, collaging, making shell mandalas, gardening, cooking—anything that lets you get into the state of flow.

This ritual involves a tea recipe to inspire and enliven your creative side and a spell to banish doubt and allow you to speak your truth.

RECIPE: For 3-4 cups of water, use 1 teaspoon each chamomile, rose hips, and orange peel, and 1/2 teaspoon each of lemon balm and lavender.

If you're daring, you'll make your tea the old witchy way by putting it out in the sun for a couple of hours to brew. Sun Tea! Drink at your own risk! If you want to make safer tea, do this:

Cold Brew: Put tea and purified water in the fridge for 6-12 hours. Serve cold.

Hot Brew: Pour boiling water over your tea. Wait a few minutes, strain if you like.

For the Creativity Spell: Light 5 tea light candles around the image of a pentagram. With a pen, pencil, spoon, or other wand of creativity, trace the pentagram in a banishing direction, starting at the bottom left, then to the top, and continuing around all 5 candles. As you do this, say and feel, "I banish all criticism, doubt, and judgment from myself and from others."

Trace around the other way in an invoking direction, starting at the top, and going down to the bottom left, then continuing over all 5 points. As you do this, say and feel, "May I be blessed with the ability to express my truth, voice, and creativity." Then drink your tea and go create something!

July 2019

	SUNDAY	MONDAY	TUESDAY
	30	1	2 ● New Moon
	7	8	9 ◗ First Quarter
	14	15	16 ○ Full Moon
	21	22	23
	28	29	30

WEDNESDAY	THURSDAY	FRIDAY	SATURDAY
Pale Blues, Grey, & Beige / Sandstone Creativity & Happiness / Hagstone Protection & Magic			
3	4	5	6
10	11	12	13
17	18	19	20
24 ◗ Last Quarter	25	26	27
31 ● New Moon	1		3

July 2019

MONDAY, JULY 1
▶ Moon void-of-course begins 5:47 PM EST
Moon enters Cancer ♋ 8:23 PM EST

TUESDAY, JULY 2
● New Moon 3:16 PM EST

WEDNESDAY, JULY 3
▶ Moon void-of-course begins 10:24 AM EST
Moon enters Leo ♌ 11:19 PM EST

THURSDAY, JULY 4

FRIDAY, JULY 5
▶ Moon void-of-course begins 2:24 PM EST

SATURDAY, JULY 6
Moon enters Virgo ♍ 12:25 AM EST

SUNDAY, JULY 7
▶ Moon void-of-course begins 12:50 PM EST
☿℞ Mercury Retrograde 7:14 PM - 7/31/19

Sea Salt - Purification

Seashells - Protection

Kyanite - Protection & Positive Energy

July 2019

MONDAY, JULY 8
Moon enters Libra ♎ 2:06 AM EST

TUESDAY, JULY 9
◑ First Quarter 6:54 AM EST
▶ Moon void-of-course begins 3:35 PM EST

WEDNESDAY, JULY 10
Moon enters Scorpio ♏ 5:28 AM EST

THURSDAY, JULY 11
▶ Moon void-of-course begins 8:28 PM EST

FRIDAY, JULY 12
Moon enters Sagittarius ♐ 11:04 AM EST

SATURDAY, JULY 13
▶ Moon void-of-course begins 9:30 PM EST

SUNDAY, JULY 14
Moon enters Capricorn ♑ 7:04 PM EST

Seawater - Use in spells for new beginnings

July 2019

*View the Full Moon through a Hagstone
and catch a glimpse of your future*

MONDAY, JULY 15

TUESDAY, JULY 16
○ Full Moon 5:38 PM EST
▶ Moon void-of-course begins 5:38 PM EST

WEDNESDAY, JULY 17
Moon enters Aquarius ♒ 5:18 AM EST

THURSDAY, JULY 18
▶ Moon void-of-course begins 11:53 AM EST

FRIDAY, JULY 19
Moon enters Pisces ♓ 5:18 PM EST

SATURDAY, JULY 20

SUNDAY, JULY 21

July 2019

MONDAY, JULY 22
▶ Moon void-of-course begins 4:34 AM EST
Moon enters Aries ♈ 6:02 AM EST

TUESDAY, JULY 23
☼ Sun enters Leo

WEDNESDAY, JULY 24
▶ Moon void-of-course begins 10:47 AM EST
Moon enters Taurus ♉ 5:42 PM EST
◑ Last Quarter 9:17 PM EST

THURSDAY, JULY 25

FRIDAY, JULY 26

SATURDAY, JULY 27
▶ Moon void-of-course begins 12:27 AM EST
Moon enters Gemini ♊ 2:28 AM EST

SUNDAY, JULY 28
▶ Moon void-of-course begins 11:23 AM EST

Bless Yourself

IN A BODY OF WATER

July · August 2019

MONDAY, JULY 29
Moon enters Cancer ♋ 7:30 AM EST

TUESDAY, JULY 30
▶ Moon void-of-course begins 11:32 PM EST

WEDNESDAY, JULY 31
Moon enters Leo ♌ 9:18 AM EST
● New Moon 11:11 PM EST
☿ Mercury goes Direct 11:58 PM

THURSDAY, AUGUST 1
▶ Moon void-of-course begins 4:47 PM EST
☆ LUGHNASADH
*Fixed Festival Date

FRIDAY, AUGUST 2
Moon enters Virgo ♍ 9:20 AM EST

SATURDAY, AUGUST 3

SUNDAY, AUGUST 4
▶ Moon void-of-course begins 12:27 AM EST
Moon enters Libra ♎ 9:29 AM EST

Blue Quartz - Spiritual Depth

Blue Opal
Spiritual Purpose

Ash - Protection & Prosperity

Seaglass - Transformation

INTUITION:

REFLECTION:

VISION & INTENTION:

IMPORTANT THINGS:

GOALS:

Wheat - Abundance

Amaranth
Health & Protection

August

MOON ENERGY AND SPELL IDEAS

NEW & WAXING MOON: Increasing abundance, success, playfulness, and fulfillment.
FULL MOON: Connecting to your guiding light and intuition. Gratitude and protection.
WANING & DARK MOON: Releasing feelings of scarcity, unworthiness, or boredom.

Sodalite
Enlightened State of Mind

Lapis Lazuli

Spiritual Power

Blue Sapphire
Expressing Your Truth

Alder - Life, confidence, & spiritual growth

Broom Craft
Moon Spells for the First Harvest

August marks the midpoint of the light half of the year. The first of three harvest festivals, known as Lughnasadh, takes place in August.

TAKING STOCK: Look back at the elemental compass that you created in February. Do you match up energetically, or are you getting closer? Does it still feel relevant and true to your highest self? If not, adjust it! What about your Ostarta Intentions? Are you taking inspired action? Are your goals still on track with what you truly desire? Are you stuck? If so, why? Think about it now. There's still time to accomplish more or change direction this year.

BESOM CRAFTING: Tie up twigs or herbs that represent protection, luck, and abundance; things like wheat, corn, flax, hazel, or elder. Decorate with sprigs of heather, basil, fennel, gorse, or borage. Add a sunflower and pendant of aventurine or tiger's eye. Consecrate your besom by running it through incense smoke or the light of a candle. Then try these spells:

Waxing Moon: Start at the edge of the room and spiral in towards the center, sweeping energetically above the floor, clockwise. Visualize, feel, and sweep in abundance and luck. Allow yourself to receive and say, "I am worthy."

Full Moon: Starting at the center of room and spiraling outwards counterclockwise. Focus on gratitude and say, "Thank you!"

Waning Moon: Starting at the center of room and spiraling outwards counterclockwise, focus on protection and sweeping away any bad energy, negativity, or anything you want to move on from. Say, "Goodbye!"

Spirituality & Psychic Powers

Borage

Basil & Dill
Protection & Abundance

Lughnasadh

A Ritual Harvest Festival
Giving Thanks for the Earth's Abundance

Lughnasadh celebrates the first of three traditional harvest festivals, a "thanksgiving" of bread and grains like corn, wheat, and millet.

The most traditional thing to do is to bake your own bread and then eat it in a ritual, however, there are plenty of twists you can take on this, like drinking beer at sunset, or eating pancakes or corn tortillas with butter and honey.

For a bread ritual, plan a picnic with a hearty seeded bread and white wine (or white tea). Use candles, bells, incense and other accoutrements if you desire, or just keep it simple with your witchy snacks and intentions of gratitude.

As you break your bread, give thanks to the sun, the earth, and the great spirit (or whoever you work with) for all that has manifested so far this year. Ask for a blessing of the next few months as the harvest season continues, and on into the dark season when winter falls. "Give back" by pouring a bit of wine (or tea) onto the earth or by scattering seeds.

You can also make some witchy herbal popcorn or sweet popcorn balls to celebrate the season. Try making sweet "abundance" balls with cinnamon, sugar, nutmeg, and butter or savory "protection and purification" popcorn with ginger, turmeric, lemon, salt, and honey. Set aside some plain, unsalted, unbuttered popcorn, seeds, or nuts for birds and animals.

It's also an excellent time to "give back" in the form of money, time, or food donations in your local community, or by meditating or working with the powers of abundance and gratitude on the metaphysical plane.

August 2019

	SUNDAY	MONDAY	TUESDAY
	28	29	30
	4	5	6
	11	12	13
	18	19	20
	25	26	27

WEDNESDAY	THURSDAY	FRIDAY	SATURDAY
31 ● New Moon	1 ☆ **LUGHNASADH** *Fixed Festival Date	2	3
☼ **LUGHNASADH** *Astronomical Date 7 ◗ First Quarter	8	9	10
14	15 ○ Full Moon	16	17
21	22	23 ◑ Last Quarter	24
28	29	30 ● New Moon	31

Purple & Blue

Gold & Brown

August 2019

MONDAY, AUGUST 5

TUESDAY, AUGUST 6
▶ Moon void-of-course begins 3:35 AM EST
Moon enters Scorpio ♏ 11:31 AM EST

WEDNESDAY, AUGUST 7
◑ First Quarter 1:30 PM EST
☼ LUGHNASADH
*Astronomical Date

THURSDAY, AUGUST 8
Moon void-of-course begins 10:57 AM EST
Moon enters Sagittarius ♐ 4:34 PM EST

FRIDAY, AUGUST 9

SATURDAY, AUGUST 10
▶ Moon void-of-course begins 3:50 PM EST

SUNDAY, AUGUST 11
Moon enters Capricorn ♑ 12:49 AM EST
♃ Jupiter goes Direct 9:37 AM
♅℞ Uranus Retrograde 10:27 PM - 1/10/20

Horse
Power & Stamina

August 2019

MONDAY, AUGUST 12
▶ Moon void-of-course begins 6:11 PM EST

TUESDAY, AUGUST 13
Moon enters Aquarius ♒ 11:35 AM EST

WEDNESDAY, AUGUST 14

THURSDAY, AUGUST 15
○ Full Moon 8:29 AM EST
▶ Moon void-of-course begins 9:01 PM EST
Moon enters Pisces ♓ 11:49 PM EST

FRIDAY, AUGUST 16

SATURDAY, AUGUST 17
▶ Moon void-of-course begins 6:34 PM EST

SUNDAY, AUGUST 18
Moon enters Aries ♈ 12:32 PM EST

Lizard – Dreams & Hidden Messages

Sweetgrass – Positive Energy

August 2019

MONDAY, AUGUST 19

TUESDAY, AUGUST 20

WEDNESDAY, AUGUST 21
▶ Moon void-of-course begins 12:06 AM EST
Moon enters Taurus ♉ 12:36 AM EST

THURSDAY, AUGUST 22
▶ Moon void-of-course begins 5:32 PM EST

FRIDAY, AUGUST 23
☼ Sun enters Virgo ♍
Moon enters Gemini ♊ 10:33 AM EST
◑ Last Quarter 10:55 AM EST

SATURDAY, AUGUST 24

SUNDAY, AUGUST 25
▶ Moon void-of-course begins 2:58 AM EST
Moon enters Cancer ♋ 5:05 PM EST

August / September 2019

MONDAY, AUGUST 26

TUESDAY, AUGUST 27
▶ Moon void-of-course begins 4:55 AM EST
Moon enters Leo ♌ 7:53 PM EST

WEDNESDAY, AUGUST 28
▶ Moon void-of-course begins 8:06 PM EST

Sparrow
Happiness & Productivity

THURSDAY, AUGUST 29
Moon enters Virgo ♍ 7:57 PM EST

FRIDAY, AUGUST 30
● New Moon 6:37 AM EST

SATURDAY, AUGUST 31
▶ Moon void-of-course begins 4:46 AM EST
Moon enters Libra ♎ 7:07 PM EST

SUNDAY, SEPTEMBER 1

INTUITION:

REFLECTION:

VISION & INTENTION:

IMPORTANT THINGS:

GOALS:

Apples - Healing & Immortality

September

MOON ENERGY AND SPELL IDEAS

NEW & WAXING MOON: Accepting loss. Recovering from grief. Preparing for change.
FULL MOON: Assessment and balance. Finding courage to make change, transform, or let go.
WANING & DARK MOON: Releasing bitterness, attachment, and things that no longer serve you.

Violet Fluorite

Stimulates the Third Eye

Hyssop
Purification

FALL CRAFT AND TEA
EMBODYING THE WITCHY AUTUMN SPIRIT

The season of autumn or fall begins in September, and so does the "offical" hot tea, cooking, baking, and crafting season. Crafts, tea, and delicious snacks give us comfort and warmth during the dark months, and for many ancient people (and some still today), winter survival depended on fall preparations.

It's a magical time to honor the abundance and blessing of food, and to cook, can things, collect herbs, make jam, and fill your pantry (or your heart!) with the fruits of the harvest.

FALL TEA: Brew an herbal tea to welcome in fall. Try an apple-spice tea or a concoction of black tea, blackberries, and sage.

FALL SCENTS: Burn incense or essential oils of frankincense, myrrh, cloves, and sandalwood.

FALL CRAFTS: Make fall candles anointed with olive or clove oil and a few drops of vanilla, then roll them in herbs like cinnamon, nutmeg, ginger, and sandalwood.

Collect inspiration for winter needlecraft and yarn projects or start planning for Samhain.

If you've got a lot of herbs harvested in late summer and early fall, make soup wreaths! Twist a 3-5 inch ring of herbs like rosemary, green onions, basil leaves, thyme, and a little bit of oregano, sage, or bay, and wrap it tightly with undyed twine. Hang to dry for a couple of weeks, then save or use in a pot of simmering soup, removing what's left when the soup is done.

FALL BAKING: Apples signify life, power, and magic! Make apple pies, apple fritters, apple butter, apple-cinnamon oatmeal, apple sauce, and spiced apple cider.

Gourd - Protection & Divination

Autumnal Equinox Rain

Collect and use in spells for releasing, banishing, and letting go.

Mabon

CAULDRON OF CHANGES
A RITUAL TO LET SOMETHING GO

Mabon, the Autumnal Equinox and start of the fall, is the second harvest festival, and the time where nature is lined up to let things go. Change is hard—and the power of autumn's cutting, falling, and decaying energy can help make necessary change happen as easily as possible.

You'll Need: A small cast-iron cauldron, or mini pumpkin carved out as a cauldron, placed on a fire-safe dish. A handful of dried sage or bay leaves and another handful of energy-clearing herbs, such as yerba santa, sweetgrass, frankincense, or sandalwood. A piece of rutilated quartz to aid in spiritual balance and releasing the past. A small scrap of paper, a pen or pencil. Think about what you want to change.

Performing the Ritual: Light several leaves of dried herb aflame in the cauldron. Set your intention to let go of whatever it is. Write it down, in as few words as possible.

Say, "Even though I might feel afraid (or whatever it is you feel) to make this change, I know it's the right thing for me to do." Stoke your cauldron flame with more herbs.

Take a moment to feel the pain or fear of letting go. Often the reluctance to feel those initial feelings is part of why it's so hard. Take a lot of deep breaths, and say the above again until your emotions shift.

Then rip up the paper. Say, "I release this, and I welcome what's next. And so it is."

Place the small bits of paper in the cauldron and watch them burn. Divine the smoke for any shapes or messages that may appear.

This spell is also excellent for Samhain.

September 2019

	SUNDAY	MONDAY	TUESDAY
	1	2	3
	8	9	10
	15	16	17
	22	23 ☆ MABON	24
	29	30	1

Wednesday	Thursday	Friday	Saturday
4	5 ◑ First Quarter	6	7
11	12	13	14 ○ Full Moon
18	19	20	21 ◑ Last Quarter
25	26	27	28 ● New Moon
2	3	4	

Red, Orange, Purple, & Brown

September 2019

MONDAY, SEPTEMBER 2
▶ Moon void-of-course begins 4:33 AM EST
Moon enters Scorpio ♏ 7:34 PM EST

TUESDAY, SEPTEMBER 3

WEDNESDAY, SEPTEMBER 4
▶ Moon void-of-course begins 6:58 AM EST
Moon enters Sagittarius ♐ 11:07 PM EST

THURSDAY, SEPTEMBER 5
◗ First Quarter 11:10 PM EST

FRIDAY, SEPTEMBER 6
▶ Moon void-of-course begins 12:03 PM EST

SATURDAY, SEPTEMBER 7
Moon enters Capricorn ♑ 6:37 AM EST

SUNDAY, SEPTEMBER 8

Sunflower ~ Wishes & Wisdom

September 2019

MONDAY, SEPTEMBER 9
▶ Moon void-of-course begins 4:33 AM EST
Moon enters Aquarius ♒ 5:23 PM EST

TUESDAY, SEPTEMBER 10

WEDNESDAY, SEPTEMBER 11
▶ Moon void-of-course begins 1:22 AM EST

THURSDAY, SEPTEMBER 12
Moon enters Pisces ♓ 5:51 AM EST

FRIDAY, SEPTEMBER 13

SATURDAY, SEPTEMBER 14
○ Full Moon 12:32 AM EST
Moon enters Aries ♈ 6:32 PM EST

SUNDAY, SEPTEMBER 15

September 2019

MONDAY, SEPTEMBER 16
▶ Moon void-of-course begins 12:02 PM EST

TUESDAY, SEPTEMBER 17
Moon enters Taurus ♉ 6:30 AM EST

WEDNESDAY, SEPTEMBER 18
♄ Saturn goes Direct 4:47 AM

THURSDAY, SEPTEMBER 19
▶ Moon void-of-course begins 9:56 AM EST
Moon enters Gemini ♊ 4:57 PM EST

FRIDAY, SEPTEMBER 20

SATURDAY, SEPTEMBER 21
◑ Last Quarter 10:40 PM EST
▶ Moon void-of-course begins 10:40 PM EST

SUNDAY, SEPTEMBER 22
Moon enters Cancer ♋ 12:49 AM EST

Squirrel - Preparedness

September 2019

MONDAY, SEPTEMBER 23
☼ Sun enters Libra ♎
▶ Moon void-of-course begins 6:05 PM EST
☆ **MABON**
Autumnal Equinox

TUESDAY, SEPTEMBER 24
Moon enters Leo ♌ 5:19 AM EST

WEDNESDAY, SEPTEMBER 25
▶ Moon void-of-course begins 12:13 PM EST

THURSDAY, SEPTEMBER 26
Moon enters Virgo ♍ 6:36 AM EST

FRIDAY, SEPTEMBER 27
▶ Moon void-of-course begins 11:57 PM EST

SATURDAY, SEPTEMBER 28
Moon enters Libra ♎ 6:02 AM EST
● New Moon 2:26 PM EST

SUNDAY, SEPTEMBER 29
▶ Moon void-of-course begins 10:05 PM EST

Acorn, Money, & Protection

September / October 2019

MONDAY, SEPTEMBER 30
Moon enters Scorpio ♏ 5:41 AM EST

Ask: What lessons have you learned?

TUESDAY, OCTOBER 1

WEDNESDAY, OCTOBER 2
▶ Moon void-of-course begins 5:45 AM EST
Moon enters Sagittarius ♐ 7:44 AM EST

THURSDAY, OCTOBER 3

FRIDAY, OCTOBER 4
▶ Moon void-of-course begins 3:33 AM EST
Moon enters Capricorn ♑ 1:25 PM EST

SATURDAY, OCTOBER 5
◐ First Quarter 12:46 PM EST

SUNDAY, OCTOBER 6
▶ Moon void-of-course begins 7:25 PM EST
Moon enters Aquarius ♒ 11:41 PM EST

HARVEST

Grapes - Prosperity

Blackbird
Psychic Awareness

Elderberry
Protection & Health

Pomegranate - Divination & Wishes

INTUITION:

REFLECTION:

VISION & INTENTION:

IMPORTANT THINGS:

Pumpkins
Magic

GOALS:

Crone & Cat
MOON FARMING COLLECTIVE

PUMPKINS · GOURDS · APPLES

October

MOON ENERGY AND SPELL IDEAS

NEW & WAXING MOON: Learning and healing from the past. Increasing psychic awareness.
FULL MOON: Transformation and divining messages from ancestors and spirit guides.
WANING & DARK MOON: Release from old emotional patterns, beliefs, and attachments.

Shadow Lanterns
Pumpkin Carving to Honor Your Dark Side

It's no coincidence that Samhain, also known as Halloween, the darkest of the witch festivals, is one that has stuck around and engrained itself in popular culture. There's a deep need for us as humans to recognize death, dying, our own mortality, and our own dark sides—the spiral of life, death, and rebirth.

Halloween's lasting presence is also a testament to the power, the presence, and the name of the Witch—the mystical practice, the lifestyle, and the magical path that is yours to celebrate and walk.

This spell puts a twist on "traditional" pumpkin carving by creating the face of your shadow self.

So, what's your problem?! Are you afraid of everything? Carve a frightened Shadow Lantern. Do you have an anger issue?! Carve an angry

jack-o-lantern to express your shadow side. Or are you passive aggressive?! Carve a pumpkin face with a wicked side-eye.

Then, light up this fun little candle spell inside your jack-o-lantern on Halloween Night.

Anoint a white candle with clove or olive oil, then roll it in purification and protection incense, such as sage, copal, sandalwood, and sweetgrass. Light the candle in your Shadow Lantern to signify the light inside that will guide you through the darkness, and that despite any darkness, you are pure light in your heart.

Or you can reverse the spell and carve a face of happiness or gratitude, then light a black candle inside to signify that although we are heading into the dark half of the year, you will keep shining and being magical.

Moonstone
Intuition

Jet - Protection & Psychic Powers

Samhain

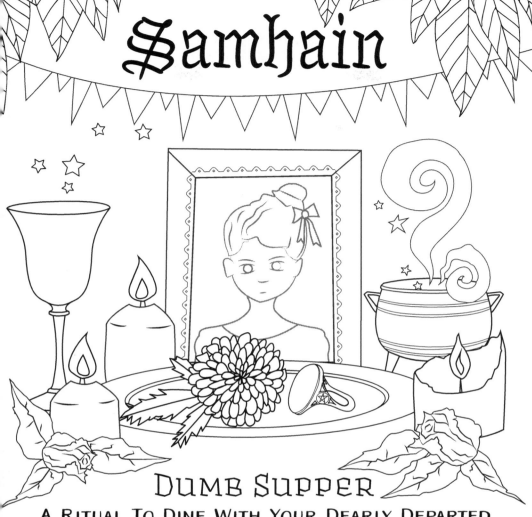

Dumb Supper
A Ritual To Dine With Your Dearly Departed

A "dumb supper" is a silent, backwards dinner to honor your loved ones who have passed on. Many cultures believe that ancestors can visit or speak to us around the time of Samhain. The veil between the living and the dead is at its thinnest, and we are more in touch with our subconscious, as well as with the spirit world, the other side, and all things mystical and mysterious.

Prepare: Sanctify your dining room with incense and invocations to clear and purify any negative energy. Set the head of the table with one place for the god, goddess, or deity of your choice and shroud the chair in an appropriately colored cloak or scarf. Then set a place at the table for each of the living, as well as each of the deceased to be remembered. Light the table only with candlelight, and place your dinner, dessert, drinks, and everything you'll need on the table. Clear the room of the living. Traditionally, you stay "deadly" silent during the dinner, However, it's your ritual, so set the "rules" as you please.

Perform the Ritual: Let everyone enter one by one, giving thanks at the place of the deity, then honoring their deceased loved one.

Have dinner backwards, starting with dessert (yay!), then dinner, salad, and appetizers last, making sure to fill the plates of your ancestors. You can substitute lit candles on their plates or pouring wine in their glasses if you prefer.

When you're finished, leave the room in the reverse order of how you came in, thanking the deity and your departed for their presence.

Once the room has been cleared, discuss any feelings, emotions, or occurrences!

October 2019

	SUNDAY	MONDAY	TUESDAY
	29	30	1
	6	7	8
	13 ○ Full Moon	14	15
	20	21 ◐ Last Quarter	22
	27 ● New Moon	28	29

Orange & Purple

Black, Brown, & Grey

WEDNESDAY	THURSDAY	FRIDAY	SATURDAY
2	3	4	5 ◑ First Quarter
9	10	11	12
16	17	18	19
23	24	25	26
30	31 ☆ SAMHAIN *Fixed Festival Date	1	

October 2019

- Witch Hazel -
Divination & Protection

MONDAY, OCTOBER 7

TUESDAY, OCTOBER 8
▶ Moon void-of-course begins 2:26 PM EST

WEDNESDAY, OCTOBER 9
Moon enters Pisces ♓ 12:05 PM EST

THURSDAY, OCTOBER 10

FRIDAY, OCTOBER 11
▶ Moon void-of-course begins 5:55 AM EST

SATURDAY, OCTOBER 12
Moon enters Aries ♈ 12:45 AM EST

SUNDAY, OCTOBER 13
○ Full Moon 5:07 PM EST
▶ Moon void-of-course begins 5:58 PM EST

October 2019

MONDAY, OCTOBER 14
Moon enters Taurus ♉ 12:23 PM EST

TUESDAY, OCTOBER 15

WEDNESDAY, OCTOBER 16
▶ Moon void-of-course begins 4:37 AM EST
Moon enters Gemini ♊ 10:29 PM EST

THURSDAY, OCTOBER 17

FRIDAY, OCTOBER 18
▶ Moon void-of-course begins 10:13 PM EST

SATURDAY, OCTOBER 19
Moon enters Cancer ♋ 6:42 AM EST

SUNDAY, OCTOBER 20

- Hemlock -
Magical Power

October 2019

MONDAY, OCTOBER 21
◑ Last Quarter 8:39 AM EST
▶ Moon void-of-course begins 8:39 AM EST
Moon enters Leo ♌ 12:28 PM EST

TUESDAY, OCTOBER 22

WEDNESDAY, OCTOBER 23
✿ Sun enters Scorpio
▶ Moon void-of-course begins 5:14 AM EST
Moon enters Virgo ♍ 3:29 PM EST

THURSDAY, OCTOBER 24

FRIDAY, OCTOBER 25
▶ Moon void-of-course begins 8:59 AM EST
Moon enters Libra ♎ 4:19 PM EST

SATURDAY, OCTOBER 26

SUNDAY, OCTOBER 27
▶ Moon void-of-course begins 4:21 AM EST
Moon enters Scorpio ♏ 4:29 PM EST
● New Moon 11:38 PM EST

- Catnip -
Good Luck

Black Cat - Magic

October · November 2019

MONDAY, OCTOBER 28

TUESDAY, OCTOBER 29
▶ Moon void-of-course begins 1:34 PM EST
Moon enters Sagittarius ♐ 5:58 PM EST

WEDNESDAY, OCTOBER 30

THURSDAY, OCTOBER 31
▶ Moon void-of-course begins 10:29 AM EST
☿℞ Mercury Retrograde 11:41 AM – 11/20/19
Moon enters Capricorn ♑ 10:38 PM EST
☆ ᛋᴀᴍʜᴀɪɴ
*Fixed Festival Date

FRIDAY, NOVEMBER 1

SATURDAY, NOVEMBER 2

SUNDAY, NOVEMBER 3
▶ Moon void-of-course begins 1:46 AM EST
Moon enters Aquarius ♒ 6:19 AM EST

INTUITION:

REFLECTION:

VISION & INTENTION:

IMPORTANT THINGS:

GOALS:

Cardamom

Nutmeg

Cloves

Black Tea

VANILLA

Cinnamon

Orange

November

MOON ENERGY AND SPELL IDEAS

NEW & WAXING MOON: Increasing coziness, comfort at home, and the simple joys of life.
FULL MOON: Interconnectedness and spiritual transcendence. Connection with others.
WANING & DARK MOON: Inward reflection. Releasing sorrow and feelings of isolation.

Ask:
Who am I? Who do I wish to be?
What do I need to know?
Where do I need to reflect?

UNDERSTANDING

GUIDANCE

Ask:
Where does spirit lead me?
What is my heart's desire?

REFLECTION

RECORDING YOUR YEAR IN YOUR BOOK OF SHADOWS

November is an awesome time to reflect and write in your Grimoire or Book of Shadows and to think back and document your magical journey so far this year.

This candle spell works with an invigorating herbal incense blend to call upon the powers of spirituality, power in mental strength, and courage. It'll also help you banish the self-doubt and internal criticism that often arises when writing and creating, allowing you to speak or write truth from your heart.

Things you'll need: A spell candle, salt, dried or fresh rosemary, and incense or essential oils of sandalwood, rosemary, and cedar. Time to write or work on your grimoire after you cast the spell!

Cast the Spell: Light your incense or diffuse the herbs as oils. Then light your spell candle.

Say your intention to spend some time writing and creating from the "flow" state of your soul.

Sprinkle salt counterclockwise around your candle in a banishing motion and say something like "With this salt, I banish all criticism, doubt, and judgment. I will now write my words of power."

Sprinkle or twirl the rosemary clockwise around the candle and say something like, "With the powers of this herb, may I be blessed with the strength and courage to speak my words of truth and wisdom. I am ready and willing. As above, so below."

Then, write or work as your candle burns. It's also empowering to cast a circle before this spell, create while you are in the circle, and then close the circle when you are finished writing.

November 2019

SUNDAY	MONDAY	TUESDAY
27 ● New Moon	28	29
3	4 ◑ First Quarter	5
10	11	12 ○ Full Moon
17	18	19 ◐ Last Quarter
24	25	26 ● New Moon

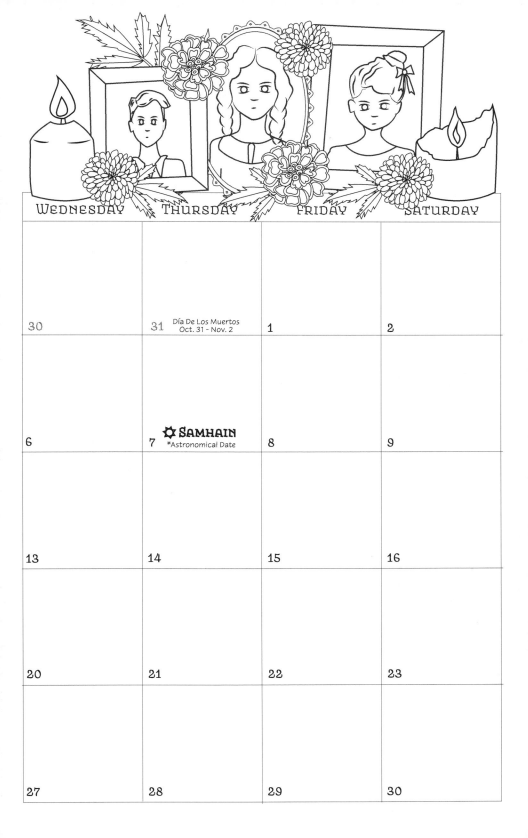

WEDNESDAY	THURSDAY	FRIDAY	SATURDAY
30	31 Día De Los Muertos Oct. 31 - Nov. 2	1	2
6	✿ **SAMHAIN** 7 *Astronomical Date	8	9
13	14	15	16
20	21	22	23
27	28	29	30

November 2019

Selenite - Spiritual Connection

MONDAY, NOVEMBER 4
◑ First Quarter 5:22 AM EST

TUESDAY, NOVEMBER 5
▶ Moon void-of-course begins 9:36 AM EST
Moon enters Pisces ♓ 6:07 PM EST

WEDNESDAY, NOVEMBER 6

THURSDAY, NOVEMBER 7
▶ Moon void-of-course begins 8:12 PM EST
✿ Samhain
*Astronomical Date

FRIDAY, NOVEMBER 8
Moon enters Aries ♈ 6:48 AM EST

SATURDAY, NOVEMBER 9

SUNDAY, NOVEMBER 10
▶ Moon void-of-course begins 9:00 AM EST
Moon enters Taurus ♉ 6:17 PM EST

November 2019

Use a wooden spoon as a wand in kitchen spells

MONDAY, NOVEMBER 11

TUESDAY, NOVEMBER 12
○ Full Moon 8:24 AM EST
▶ Moon void-of-course begins 10:47 AM EST

WEDNESDAY, NOVEMBER 13
Moon enters Gemini ♊ 3:45 AM EST

THURSDAY, NOVEMBER 14

FRIDAY, NOVEMBER 15
▶ Moon void-of-course begins 6:39 AM EST
Moon enters Cancer ♋ 11:14 AM EST

SATURDAY, NOVEMBER 16

SUNDAY, NOVEMBER 17
▶ Moon void-of-course begins 3:14 PM EST
Moon enters Leo ♌ 4:56 PM EST

November 2019

MONDAY, NOVEMBER 18

TUESDAY, NOVEMBER 19
◑ Last Quarter 4:10 PM EST
▶ Moon void-of-course begins 4:10 PM EST
Moon enters Virgo ♍ 8:54 PM EST

WEDNESDAY, NOVEMBER 20
☿ Mercury goes Direct 2:12 PM

THURSDAY, NOVEMBER 21
▶ Moon void-of-course begins 10:31 PM EST
Moon enters Libra ♎ 11:19 PM EST

FRIDAY, NOVEMBER 22
☼ Sun enters Sagittarius ♐

SATURDAY, NOVEMBER 23
▶ Moon void-of-course begins 9:49 PM EST

SUNDAY, NOVEMBER 24
Moon enters Scorpio ♏ 12:58 AM EST

White

Dark Purple

Grey

November · December 2019

MONDAY, NOVEMBER 25
▶ Moon void-of-course begins 12:29 PM EST

TUESDAY, NOVEMBER 26
Moon enters Sagittarius ♐ 3:10 AM EST
● New Moon 10:05 AM EST

WEDNESDAY, NOVEMBER 27
♆ Neptune goes Direct 7:32 AM

THURSDAY, NOVEMBER 28
▶ Moon void-of-course begins 5:49 AM EST
Moon enters Capricorn ♑ 7:32 AM EST

FRIDAY, NOVEMBER 29
▶ Moon void-of-course begins 10:56 AM EST

SATURDAY, NOVEMBER 30
Moon enters Aquarius ♒ 3:13 PM EST

SUNDAY, DECEMBER 1

INTUITION:

REFLECTION:

VISION & INTENTION:

Owls - Messages from the Other Side - Wisdom of the Dark

IMPORTANT THINGS:

GOALS:

December

MOON ENERGY AND SPELL IDEAS

NEW & WAXING MOON: Increasing rest and relaxation. Enhancing a jolly mood and spirit.
FULL MOON: Rebirth and transformation. Recognizing your brilliance and light.
WANING & DARK MOON: Releasing to the universe. Respite and surrender to the unknown.

Poinsettia
Festivity & Generosity

Mistletoe
Love, Protection, & Health

YULE GREETINGS

Carve a witchy symbol onto a potato stamp
and use it to decorate Yule cards and gifts.

Decorative Yule Spellwork
Blessing Your Tree, Log, or Greenery

The winter solstice is the longest night of the year and the shortest, darkest day. Yet it marks the turning point where the days will begin to get longer again—a cause for celebration of the sun.

Many Yule traditions involve flames and decorative indoor greenery to herald the return of light and spring, like the Yule Log, where a sanctified and decorated log is burned in the Yule fire. The Yule tree and evergreen boughs represent the everlasting life of the universe and/or deity, as they don't wither in winter, a symbol of life surviving through the dark season. And Scandinavian lore suggests using greenery indoors to give faeries and woodland spirits a warm place for the winter. Aww!

As you bring decorative greenery into your home, perform a simple consecration and blessing to set the mood and honor its presence.

You'll Need: A cauldron or incense burner and charcoal to burn frankincense and myrrh. An undecorated Yule log, tree, or altar greenery.

Casting the Spell: Begin by burning the frankincense and myrrh. Circle around your tree or log in a clockwise direction three times. If you can't circle it, you can just stand before it, or cast a circle in front of it. Say a few words to thank the spirit of the tree or greenery for its presence and sacrifice to be honored, decorated, and used in ritual for the Solstice. Bless it with the power of the elements and then chant the following ancient words, the "traditional" chant sung when the Yule Log burns on the solstice.

"May the Log Burn, May the Wheel Turn, May Evil Spurn, May the Sun Return."

Winter Solstice Snow

Collect and use in purification spells

Fir
Clarity

Garnet
Regenerative Healing

Frankincense
Spiritual Connection & Protection

Yule

Pink Topaz
Hope & Divinity

Clear Topaz
Awareness & Purification

DREAMS

JOY

PEACE

Ruby
Energy Clearing

Blue Topaz
Your Highest Self

The Winter Solstice
Celebrating the Longest Night of the Year

The winter solstice is a time of powerful magic where the sun is at its weakest and the seasons shift from dark to light. Ancient people celebrated the return of the sun at Yule. However, it's also an auspicious time to go inward and follow any quiet curiosities or intuitive nudges. It is an "in-between" time, a chance to slip into another world and change the course of your future. And since it's the darkest point of the year, it's a time where you can see, hear, and begin to incubate exciting new things that have yet to be realized.

Winter's energy is also about conserving—less on action and more on attaining knowledge, learning, and using the quiet moments to explore what might be brewing beneath the surface.

Make the most of the Solstice day by celebrating it from dawn till dusk.

AT SUNRISE: Go outside before dawn and greet the first rays of sunlight. Light a fire or candles to help encourage the sun (since it's at its weakest). Ring bells and cheer when it arrives. Drink hot cider, tea, spiced wine, or wassail, and "pour libations" to the earth as an offering.

AT NOON: Do tarot and divination. Try slow, wintery things like tea leaf-reading or scrying into a glass ornament, fireplace, or candle. Or pull tarot cards and ask questions to find clues to what you want to bring to light next.

AT SUNSET: Time to feast and be merry! Celebrate the sun's light, your own light within, and all of the blessings you've received in this magical year. You made it to the darkest point of the Wheel. Celebrate and welcome back the sun.

December 2019

SUNDAY	MONDAY	TUESDAY
1	2	3
8	9	10
15	16	17
22	23	24
29	30	31

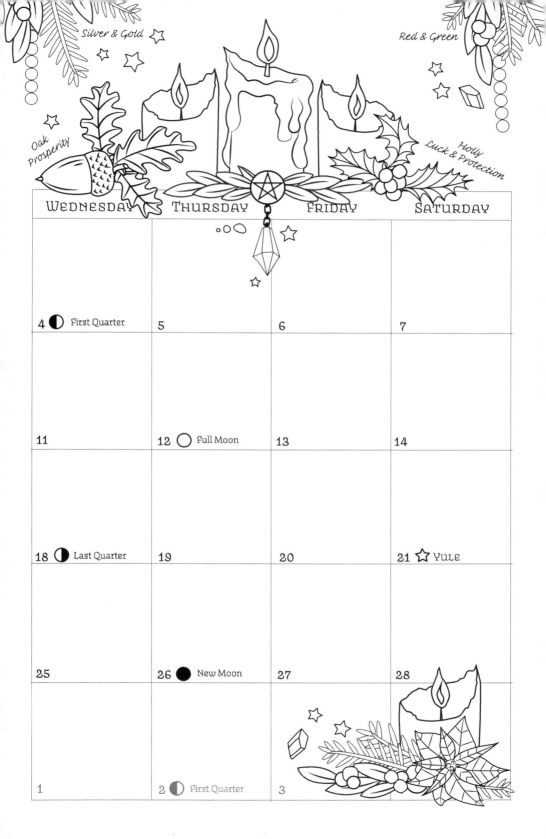

Silver & Gold

Red & Green

Oak Prosperity

Holly Luck & Protection

WEDNESDAY	THURSDAY	FRIDAY	SATURDAY
4 ◑ First Quarter	5	6	7
11	12 ○ Full Moon	13	14
18 ◐ Last Quarter	19	20	21 ☆ YULE
25	26 ● New Moon	27	28
1	2 ◑ First Quarter	3	

December 2019

MONDAY, DECEMBER 2
▶ Moon void-of-course begins 7:27 AM EST

TUESDAY, DECEMBER 3
Moon enters Pisces ♓ 2:10 AM EST

WEDNESDAY, DECEMBER 4
◖ First Quarter 1:58 AM EST

THURSDAY, DECEMBER 5
▶ Moon void-of-course begins 3:14 AM EST
Moon enters Aries ♈ 2:44 PM EST

FRIDAY, DECEMBER 6

SATURDAY, DECEMBER 7
▶ Moon void-of-course begins 10:01 AM EST

SUNDAY, DECEMBER 8
Moon enters Taurus ♉ 2:29 AM EST

Plum Pudding

December 2019

MONDAY, DECEMBER 9
▶ Moon void-of-course begins 8:12 PM EST

TUESDAY, DECEMBER 10
Moon enters Gemini ♊ 11:46 AM EST

WEDNESDAY, DECEMBER 11

THURSDAY, DECEMBER 12
◯ Full Moon 12:12 AM EST
▶ Moon void-of-course begins 12:12 AM EST
Moon enters Cancer ♋ 6:22 PM EST

FRIDAY, DECEMBER 13

SATURDAY, DECEMBER 14
▶ Moon void-of-course begins 10:56 AM EST
Moon enters Leo ♌ 10:55 PM EST

SUNDAY, DECEMBER 15

December 2019

MONDAY, DECEMBER 16
▶ Moon void-of-course begins 5:09 PM EST

TUESDAY, DECEMBER 17
Moon enters Virgo ♍ 2:15 AM EST

WEDNESDAY, DECEMBER 18
◐ Last Quarter 11:56 PM EST

THURSDAY, DECEMBER 19
▶ Moon void-of-course begins 3:06 AM EST
Moon enters Libra ♎ 5:04 AM EST

FRIDAY, DECEMBER 20

SATURDAY, DECEMBER 21
▶ Moon void-of-course begins 6:45 AM EST
Moon enters Scorpio ♏ 7:57 AM EST
☆ Yule - Winter Solstice

SUNDAY, DECEMBER 22
✸ Sun enters Capricorn ♑
▶ Moon void-of-course begins 10:27 AM EST

December 2019

MONDAY, DECEMBER 23
Moon enters Sagittarius ♐ 11:34 AM EST

TUESDAY, DECEMBER 24

WEDNESDAY, DECEMBER 25
▶ Moon void-of-course begins 6:18 AM EST
Moon enters Capricorn ♑ 4:45 PM EST

THURSDAY, DECEMBER 26
● New Moon 12:12 AM EST

FRIDAY, DECEMBER 27
▶ Moon void-of-course begins 4:02 PM EST

SATURDAY, DECEMBER 28
Moon enters Aquarius ♒ 12:20 AM EST

SUNDAY, DECEMBER 29

Christmas Cactus
Hope Amidst Darkness

December 2019 / January 2020

MONDAY, DECEMBER 30
▶ Moon void-of-course begins 5:23 AM EST
Moon enters Pisces ♓ 10:41 AM EST

TUESDAY, DECEMBER 31

WEDNESDAY, JANUARY 1
▶ Moon void-of-course begins 9:13 PM EST
Moon enters Aries ♈ 11:00 PM EST

THURSDAY, JANUARY 2
◑ First Quarter 11:45 PM EST

FRIDAY, JANUARY 3
▶ Moon void-of-course begins 8:18 PM EST

SATURDAY, JANUARY 4
Moon enters Taurus ♉ 11:15 AM EST

SUNDAY, JANUARY 5

Wassail
Good Health

About the Artist

Amy Cesari
(and her familiar, Cornelius)

Amy is a forest dwelling Author and Illustrator. She's also an avid crocheter, gardener, and has a ridiculously goofy sense of humor. Not only does she own every Nintendo game console ever made, she's earned several fancy diplomas and enjoys continued studies in various magical practices.

CONTACT AMY AND SEE MORE BOOKS, PRINTABLE PAGES, AND ART :

Amy@coloringbookofshadows.com
ColoringBookofShadows.com

Made in the USA
Middletown, DE
04 January 2019